I0617830

Makeshift Manifesto

Makeshift Manifesto

Design by James Reich

I almost wish I didn't feel compelled to do this and I apologize in advance for being an insecure, egocentric asshole.

—Christopher Merlyn
San Francisco, CA. May 2017

Makeshift Manifesto

A Life in the Day of Christopher Merlyn

Preface

This originally started with a proclamation about how I had no idea what I was doing. Which, to be fair, was true. I went on to spew about how I wanted to quit this several times, went months without looking at it, and wasn't sure if it would actually reach completion. Which was also true. I started this endeavor when I was twenty-nine and finished at thirty-three. It was riddled with typos, a lack of punctuation, and mentioned every character by their government name. This wasn't meant to be spiteful. Looking back, I think I just wanted to relay the narrative in its unadulterated form. However, five years later, I'm back to make revisions. I didn't want to lose the authenticity of the original version, as it documented the time and space that I felt inspired to bring this to fruition. So, although my writing style has (slightly) improved over the last decade, I held back.

I think I caught and fixed the typos. I polished up most of the punctuation, and I changed almost all the names. Hopefully, the people who hated me for doing this, will hate me just a little less. I could say more but my story's already written. And although I'm still here and even dare I say, progressing, the more amusing shit is in these pages. Enjoy...

Actually I don't remember being born, it must have happened during one of my blackouts.

—Jim Morrison

1

My name is Christopher Merlyn Jake Sebastian-Evans. Everybody calls me Kit. I was born at approximately six o'clock in the morning on March 1st, 1984 in a borough of London, England called, Islington. It was a leap year and I just missed February 29th by a few hours. I went home from the hospital with my mom, dad and older sister, Lisa, who came along three years before me.

I have two half brothers, Charles and Max, from my dad's previous marriage. I don't recall what our house actually looked like, I only lived there until I was about three years old. I've seen some pictures of the place but nothing that really rings a bell. It was all brick on the outside and was supposedly haunted by a really pissed off ghost. We had stairs and my mom said somebody or something used to try and push her down them, what a dick. Since I can't recall next to anything about my life and living situation at this time, I'll shed some light on the people that do. My mom was born and raised in England. My dad was originally from Wales but he went to school in London and proceeded to pursue a life and career there. My mom's family was Jewish with roots back to Austria, which by heritage makes me Jewish as fuck. Although my mom was always somewhat rebellious against her family and pretty much anything they were into. I've never practiced Hanukkah and know next to nothing about Judaism. Both my folks thought religion was kind of silly, although my dad used to make us read passages from the Bible occasionally for educational purposes. My dad was close to ten years older than my mom. He lived through World War 2, had to hang out in bomb shelters and all that crazy shit, while my mom was born right around the time the war ended. Her folks fled the country to escape the Holocaust. She might not have been born if they had stuck around.

My folks were smart; they came from old-fashioned upbringing. School was important, there may have been consequences if you didn't make the grade, at least on dad's side. I don't know as much about my mom's side because she almost never talked about them, she just didn't care to. My mom was into school though, she wanted to do well and get good grades.

I never knew any of my grandparents but I talked to my mom's folks a few times on the phone when I was a kid. She didn't seem that fazed when they passed. My folks are both college graduates. My dad attended Cambridge and my mom went to Oxford. That's like England's equivalent of Harvard and Yale. Dad studied law and mom pursued journalism. Dad went on to being a fairly successful trial lawyer and mom got a job freelancing for the BBC. So dad was in and out of court, putting folks away or getting them out (he switched sides at some point), while mom was interviewing and schmoozing with celebrities at the time. I honestly don't even know when or how the two of them met. I'm sure the story has been told to me but I can't recall. I think it was through a mutual friend.

Lisa came on the scene not too long after they were married. My mom stopped working and stepped into being a stay at home parent while dad took on the role of breadwinner. It was good for a while; my folks were financially stable once upon a time. It didn't last though, my parents are one of those had it and lost it stories. We'll go into that in a bit. Regardless of background and upbringing, my parents both got into their fair share of mischief. They dabbled with drugs throughout the 60's and 70's like everyone else. My dad more so than my mom. They both generally stuck to weed and booze though. Dad especially loved the sauce; he was an alcoholic for virtually my entire life.

Let's fast forward a little bit. My folks took a trip to San Diego, California in the early-mid-80s. They had some friends out there and back then, America was still the land of opportunity. California especially was beautiful and economically thriving. They fell in love with it and planned to move there not long after returning home. So we packed up shop and left London in search of some kind of American dream: sandy beaches, beautiful sunsets, stellar weather, Southern California. We touched down at 5335 Canterbury Drive in a cool little neighborhood called, Kensington. This was my first real recollection of home. I remember what the place looked like inside and out. It was a beautiful house. I especially loved the living room. It had crazy high ceilings. I remember being a little kid looking up at the beams holding it together, thinking if you fell from one of them, you would die.

The living room sprawled out into a dining room, which on one side, connected to the kitchen, which went through into the laundry room, which landed you in a hallway that packed three bedrooms and a bathroom. On the other side of the living room was another bedroom, an office space that went through to a two-car garage that went through to an amazing pool area, that connected to a beautiful patio, that connected to the backyard. Sounds nice, right? It was, this house was the shit. My little sister, Zoe, was born shortly after we moved in, so this was her first home. She's the only American citizen in the family.

One of my earliest and clearer memories of this house and my life in general was my fifth birthday. I had one of those inflatable bounce houses in the back yard. There was a clown there doing magic tricks, we had a huge cake, the works; it was great (at the time anyways, clowns kind of scare me now). I attended a pre school called Fleur de lis and went on to kindergarten at Francis Parker. I can't recall which one of these schools this first incident actually took place, but it turned out I was prone to having seizures as a kid and I had a bad one in class one day. I'd had others in the past, but this was the first one I actually remember. I vaguely recall falling out of my seat, being on the floor, my teachers freaking out, and waking up in the hospital. One of my teachers was actually there with me when I came to, along with some kids from my class. There were balloons tied to my hospital bed. I don't know if I had any other major scares after that but I went on to have problems with asthma. There were many times when my poor mom had to take me to the emergency room in the middle of the night because I'd wake up hacking and incapable of breathing. I'm totally smoking a cigarette while writing this.

Besides all that, my early grade school experience was pretty normal. In 1989, at age five, I started taking piano lessons with a fairly renowned instructor named Lynn. When I wasn't having lessons, I was getting schooled by my dad at home. Dad was an amazing pianist and artist. When he wasn't in court, giving seminars or writing books about advocacy, he was drawing, painting, or playing the piano. The dude was crazy talented. He was also an airplane enthusiast; he almost became a certified pilot. He had the equivalent of a permit license to fly a small plane and took me up a few times. I got airsick once and vomited all over the cockpit, it was gnarly. My dad's teaching methods were pretty hardcore compared to Lynn's. She was patient; she only lost her cool with me a couple of times. I probably deserved it.

My dad, on the other hand, would lose his cool a lot. He was usually drunk and irritable and if I made mistakes or didn't give one hundred percent, he'd occasionally go upside my head. Other times he'd throw his chair or something within arms reach across the room. He yelled a lot, I dreaded sitting down at the piano with him most of the time. I didn't have a choice though. When dad said it was time to play, it was time to play. If I really wasn't into it, I'd try and get my mom to tell him to fuck off but that usually just resulted in the two of them fighting. That was ugly every time. My folks didn't have small arguments. Their quarrels were pretty extreme. One of them would get hurt, shit would get broken, etc. My sisters and I would try to intervene sometimes but we were so young and small. Most of the time we would just hide in a closet or in the next room waiting for it to stop. My sisters had to play too; they took lessons with Lynn as well.

Although dad's teaching methods weren't always tender, they were effective. Between him and Lynn, I was playing Chopin and Mozart by the time I was seven years old. I could read pretty serious sheet music and went on to win competitions and recitals. I had awards and trophies, I was a child prodigy for a while there. My sisters too, we were all good, especially for being so young. Today, I'm not half as good as I used to be but I still love to play.

I remember on my sixth birthday, my mom gave me a poem titled *Now We Are Six*. That, for some reason, is the one thing that really stands out. My dad wasn't an asshole all the time. He was actually pretty cool when he wasn't drunk and losing his mind. He'd let me watch R-rated movies and take me to Belmont Park to blow money at the arcade. He'd take me to Padres games at Jack Murphy Stadium, he taught me how to drive his car in the parking lot after the games when everyone cleared out. He bought me my first Playboy and my first rap tape. My mom actually deserves some credit here too for buying me an MC Hammer album. I was into the *Hammer Man* cartoon, which was basically MC Hammer fighting crime with his magic shoes that enabled him to defeat bad guys with sweet dance moves. I watched that shit almost every Saturday morning. Maybe my mom actually bought me my first rap tape. But my dad (against his better judgment) bought me a Cypress Hill tape. I didn't listen to that MC Hammer album much after forming a relationship with Cypress Hill. Dad would let me listen to my tapes in his Cadillac on the way to and from school. He would tell me that he didn't like it but would support my foul taste as long as he could school me on music of his choice as well. Basically, if you want to listen to that bullshit, you have to know something about this shit too. Dad was a music lover and collector. He had records, tapes and CDs for days. So he and I would sit down, he'd pour a drink, light a smoke and play me records. Every song usually came with a descriptive rant about whatever we were listening to. Some days it was Opera or Classical, other days it was Pink Floyd, The Rolling Stones or Steely Dan. It was actually cool. I listen to all that stuff to this day (as well as MC Hammer and Cypress Hill). My mom wasn't as into music but she had her preferences. She liked the more groovy shit. Elvis Presley, The Beatles, Soul and R&B singers like Al Greene and Whitney Houston. She liked

Jazz too but being a reporter/journalist, she was usually listening to AM radio.

My folks were fighting a lot during this time, I don't know what exactly was happening or why but they seemed to always be going at it. My mom used to take us away for days at a time, usually in the middle of the night when dad was sleeping, so as to avoid further drama. We'd go stay at a friend's house or get a room somewhere. I remember thinking it was even kind of fun, like we were going on an adventure or something. I guess my mom just didn't know how to deal sometimes so occasionally she'd just run away. She always took me and my sisters with her though, she never left us with my dad. She was worried that he'd get tossed and start doing something crazy. This continued on until my seventh birthday. My folks were still on thin ice but pulled it together for the sake of the kid turning seven. We went to dinner at the Hard Rock Cafe. It was crappy, the waiter spilled a glass of water on me and the tension between my folks was building from the time we sat down. My dad proceeded to get inebriated and by the time we got home, the shit was hitting the fan. Dad swung on mom as well as thrashed the house a bit. Mom snapped and called the police.

The cops showed up fairly quickly and in a matter of minutes, dad was in bracelets and going to jail. I was hiding in my room while most of this was going down but my dad called me out to see him off. He asked the cops if he could please have a word with his son before being taken away. I went out to the living room and saw dad in handcuffs, being held by two officers. He told me to take a good look and consider it a birthday present. I'm still not totally sure what he meant by that. Maybe a life lesson about ramifications for our actions or something. Maybe he was just ripped and being dramatic. I thought about it the first time I ended up in cuffs but that's many years later. The cops took him out and put him in the car then went back inside to talk to my mom. The whole 'option to press charges' deal. My sisters and I went outside to see dad shacked up in the back of the squad car. He looked sad and a little defeated. He said he was sorry through the glass. My sisters and I started crying, I felt sorry for him, regardless of the fact that he had just ruined my birthday. I went inside and got a stuffed teddy bear from my room and asked the cops if he could please take it to jail with him. They obviously said no, probably just as well. Jail is the last place you want to be rolling up in with a teddy bear. So dad went away and the rest of us tried to continue with the night like it was all good. It was hard but I still had presents to open and my mom was determined to try and salvage the remainder of my birthday.

I don't remember exactly how long dad was locked up but I think he was out in a few days. He came home drained but happy to be out. He started attending AA shortly after that. I don't know if it was by choice or court order, probably court order, maybe both. Either way, he was trying to make the switch for a while. He took me to a couple of meetings with him. I don't know if he thought it would be a good experience for a seven year old or if he just wanted me to see that he wasn't the only one. It was strange, sitting in a circle of grown men, all strangers, listening to these personal stories about their trials and tribulations with alcohol. I remember the sympathetic dynamic between everyone. The whole, "Hi, I'm so and so and I'm an alcoholic." "Hi so and so." My dad introduced me when it was his turn to share, they all turned to me and said, "Hi Kit." Dad told them about getting arrested on my birthday.

Everyone has the right to believe anything they want. And everyone else has the right to find it fucking ridiculous.

—Ricky Gervais

2

ad's AA meetings were held in a pocket of downtown San Diego and there were always a few homeless folks around. When the meeting was over, dad and I would walk to the car and he usually made a point of throwing a homeless dude a dollar here and there. Sometimes he would make me do it. He'd stop, take a buck or some change from his coat, place it in my hand and instruct me to go give it to whatever lucky vagrant was the prize winner for that night.

The meetings worked for a while, dad stayed sober after the birthday incident and focused on work. The sisters and I had switched schools and were now attending All Saints, a private Episcopalian school (like a slightly more tolerant version of a catholic school). Like I said, we weren't religious but our parents wanted us to get an above average education if possible. We had to wear uniforms and the principal was a priest who happened to be ex military. The school was connected to a church and we had mass every Monday morning. This is where I more or less wrote off religion on my own. Although I learned and could recite the prayers, did the studies and played the game, I remember thinking it was all kind of absurd. It just didn't add up to me, I had questions and there was no room for questioning anything. I believe in a higher power and don't have any personal issues with organized religion but I think it makes people a little crazy. I have a lot of religious friends, am a big fan of religious imagery as well as think people should be able to worship and love whomever they choose. But for me, especially at the time, I just didn't take to it. What can I say, I'm the product of a lawyer and a journalist, give me some evidence. Needless to say, I didn't get it and it's difficult to sell a young kid on faith alone when it's not instilled from the beginning. So I did what most kids do, I rebelled. Not necessarily against the church or the school but just protocol in general. I was at that age and my surroundings at the time fueled my fire. I was good at it too; this was the beginning stage of a role that came pretty naturally to me. I was a class clown, an attention whore, I argued and didn't like doing homework. Sometimes I would sit in class while homework was being assigned and already start thinking of an excuse to use the next day for why I didn't do it.

I remember a kid in my French class got a pass on doing his homework once because his Grandpa passed away. A light bulb went off in my head and I decided that's a good one I hadn't used yet. So a couple weeks later I used the same excuse. It wasn't a total lie, my Grandpa was dead, he'd just been dead for a while. It worked like a charm as planned, up until that afternoon when Lisa went to the same class and the teacher said, "I'm so sorry about your

Grandpa." Lisa was confused and politely inquired as to what the hell she was talking about. That was my bad. I failed to track Lisa down and tell her that Gramps was freshly dead and if she needed an excuse for not doing her homework, it worked for me. I can't remember the French teachers name but she watched me like a hawk after that. I didn't get away with shit in that class ever again, understandably. I got popped selling a golden wolf ticket so even if the dog really did eat my homework, from that point on, nobody would have believed me.

I wasn't a straight up menace or anything, I think I was just bored by what was considered conventional. I did good work when I actually did the work and still managed to uphold decent grades. Although I struggled with math, still do. Outside of school, I was playing sports. I played soccer and baseball but eventually gave all that up for skateboarding. Belmont Park was a popular skate spot back in the day and when dad would take me there to play at the arcade, I would watch the skaters do their thing. I bugged out on those guys. I remember wondering, how the hell do they do that shit? In addition to curiosity, they just looked cool. Misfit looking kids in baggy clothes, smoking, cussing, drinking, there were usually girls hanging around. It looked fun, I wanted to get down. I got a deck and cruised around for a while but didn't try to get semi serious about it until a few years later.

I was in my dad's office the first time I heard *Another Brick in the Wall* by Pink Floyd. I think we were painting.

I remember he even said something to the affect of, "check this one out, you'll like this." That track was dope. The chorus with all the kids screaming they "don't need no education" and telling the teacher to leave them alone. That was the jam, I didn't want to go back to school after that. Around the same time, Lisa and her friends put me on a variety of things from Queen to Black Sabbath to Nirvana and my brothers had sent a recommendation to check out The Ramones and Frank Zappa. So my young mind was traveling outside the box. I was pretty much studying my own personal revolution through music. Soon after, a kid at school introduced me to N.W.A. and other rappers that were hot at the time. MTV took care of the rest at home. The 90's were a pretty great time for music. There was still a sense of revolt or weird encouragement to be different. I liked that shit. I found it inspiring. It sounds lame or typical but I suppose it's primitive. I'm 8-9 years old at this point. I can't say that music alone influenced me to be or act a certain way but it excited me. I chose to be influenced. It was a good addition to my already rebellious behavior.

Besides being captivated by music and anti heroes, the one other thing that stands out about this point in my life (I think) is Fibermesh.

Fibermesh was the name of a case that my dad was working on. It was a big one. It consumed his work life as well as the firm he was working for at the time. This case actually led to him falling off the wagon and he started drinking again after a good run with sobriety. I didn't know at the time but the case was a make or break. If he had won, we probably would have been well off for a minute. But he didn't win, the poor bastard lost and the dominoes started falling from there.

I can't ask my dad how or why things went down the way they did because he's been dead for a while now. I don't talk to my mom about anything pertaining to him or the situation because she just gets mad. But I think after the case was settled, things took a turn for the worst and his firm basically let him go. Amidst all this craziness, my folks decided to split town for a moment. I'm not sure if they had a plan or just needed a breather but either way they chose to hit the road. I'm not sure how the decision came about but when it was all said and done, they decided on New Mexico.

The kids didn't really know what was going on, we just figured we were taking a vacation. I vaguely remember mom had mentioned she wanted to visit Santa Fe so we packed our bags and bounced out for a week.

We flew into Albuquerque, rented a car and drove an hour north to Santa Fe where we checked into a little motel on Cerrillos road. It was like a small apartment with a kitchenette, not a bad setup for someone staying an extended period of time. It was in what I would consider midtown, meaning that it wasn't super cheap but definitely wasn't some fancy downtown hotel. Santa Fe was pretty cool, it was different, rich in culture and everyone seemed friendly for the most part. It was small too so it was easy to get around as a visitor. My folks loved it, I guess they were getting older and having lived in cities for the better part of their lives, the small town vibe was appealing.

They also had some old friends from back in England who happened to live down in Albuquerque: a nice couple from a similar background, Charles and Yvonne. Charles was a trial lawyer and Yvonne was a doctor of alternative medicine. My mom had been getting into all that and Santa Fe was a mecca for alternative healers.

Can you guess where this is going? Yeah, whoopedi-fucking doo kids, we're moving to New Mexico.

I get it, it's new, it's different, it's time for change. Dad's out of work and Charles says he could maybe get him in with a firm out there. Mom's mesmerized by the possibilities of this, that and the other. The people are so nice and it's beautiful. They get all four fucking seasons in New Mexico (which basically just means it's cold six months out of the year). It seems like a great place to raise kids, I guess. There's also no beach. I understand that the pros are currently outweighing the cons but dude, no beach.

So we head back to San Diego and get the ball rolling on the big move. I say goodbye to my friends, my school, my awesome house with the pool and high ceilings, my piano teacher and my neighborhood. I'm about to turn ten.

When Brian told me that he grew up in New Mexico, I said I thought it was cool that people from other countries played football. He corrected me on my geography and agreed to sit down with me anyway.

—Terry Bradshaw

3

We touched down in New Mexico and ended up renting a place on the outskirts of Santa Fe in the middle of fucking nowhere. I don't know why my folks chose this place, guess it seemed like a good idea at the time. Maybe the price was right seeing as their financial status was in transition. It was on several acres of land, which was pretty but seriously in the cut. The house was alright but poorly built and frequently had problems. We had mice, crazy ass spiders, and I almost stepped on a rattlesnake once, barefoot, outside the front door. There was a general store down the way that basically serviced the whole community out there and if you needed anything else, you had to drive 20-30 minutes into town. The school I was fitting to attend was close though, it also happened to be just down the way from the state penitentiary. This was the first public school I attended. The sisters and I all switched to public schools at some point. This academic cesspool was Turquoise Trail Elementary, this place sucked. The kids all had some kind of chip on their shoulder, they weren't friendly or welcoming and they treated me like exactly what I was, an outsider.

To make matters more interesting, for the first time in

my life, I was a minority. Everyone was Latino or Native American and evidently weren't crazy about white kids. I got messed with from the minute I walked in the door. I'd never experienced racial discrimination before then. My school back in California was pretty diverse; there were white kids, black kids, Mexican kids, East Indian and Asian kids. I imagine if you racially bashed someone, it would have been an issue. Wasn't the case here, the authorities had bigger problems. Kids were fighting, bringing weapons to school, telling the teachers off, etc. So I adjusted and got used to being called *guerro, white boy, puto, gringo* and all the other things they'd say to make me feel good about myself. I made a couple of friends but for the most part, I tried to keep my head down and keep to myself. I wasn't as mischievous as I was back in California, probably because my confidence was down and I was hesitant to attract attention to myself.

I hated lunch and I hated recess, it was always drama. Some little asshole gangbanger in training was always coming up to me in line asking what I claimed. Then you'd get on the playground and they would be in your face asking if you were looking at them when you clearly weren't. This environment gradually made me angry. I grew tired of this bullshit, eventually snapped and got in my first fight at that school. It wasn't a bad scrap but I'd say I lost.

I remember a kid from my class pulled a knife on a teacher once. He actually got expelled. Shortly after that incident, another kid threatened to attempt suicide at recess. There was a big water tower at the end of the playground. He hopped the fence that separated it from school property, climbed up to the top of it and threatened to jump. They shut the school down but I remember his mom showed up and started yelling at him from the ground in a pretty hostile manner. I'm no expert but if there was ever a time to not yell at your kid, that would probably be it.

A few weeks later I heard the same kid's mom actually died in a tragic accident. I don't know if this is true but it was word around the halls. She was supposedly boning some dude in his car, parked at a look out point. They accidentally bumped the car into neutral and rolled off a cliff. How do you explain something like that to a 10-year-old? Anyways, these were the kids I went to school with.

During this time at home, things were so-so. Mom and dad were still having their occasional issues while trying to adjust to new surroundings and my sisters were dealing with the same scenario in their own way. I think we all missed California, my sisters and I would talk on the phone with friends back home frequently. Six months or so passed and we eventually moved into town, thank God. My folks grew tired of the inconveniences of living in the middle of nowhere and packed up shop to get closer to civilization. This was awesome because it meant I got to switch schools. I didn't know what I was in for, I just knew it couldn't be worse than where I already was.

Moving into town made me hate New Mexico less. Our

house was better, the surroundings were better and my school wasn't the seventh circle of Hell. I'm now attending Acequia Madre Elementary. A public school in a nice part of town with a little more diversity. I got along with more of the kids here, I got back into sports a little bit as well as my more confident, mischievous manner. I did alright here though, I upheld good grades and was overall content. I actually met kids at this school that I still keep in touch with today. Two things immediately stand out about this time in my life. My sixth grade teacher had a heart attack in the middle of class and blamed it on us, seriously. Veteran teacher of thirty plus years and we supposedly retired him. He quit teaching after that. And the other thing is my twelfth birthday.

This is going to sound ridiculous, but my twelfth birthday party was kind of legendary. My parents were away for the night and Lisa, who was a troublesome teenager at this point, decided to throw me a party at the house. She'd been a freshman at Santa Fe High for a minute and had meshed with all kinds of folks. Hip Hop kids, Goths, Hippies, she put the word out and it spread like a plague. One thing led to another and by the middle of the night, the house was upside down. There were kids everywhere, drinking, smoking, skateboarding in the house, doing drugs in the bathroom, making out on the couch, puking off the roof; it was madness. When shit started getting nuts, I actually bailed up the street with a couple friends from school to go skate. My boy, Coley, was an awesome skateboarder, really good for his age. All he wanted to do was skate, so we dipped. I had fun too, night skating was a blast back then. By the time we got back, the place was pretty thrashed. Almost everyone had left (I think the cops got called), Lisa was faded but kind of going into panic mode. The party got way out of hand and our parents were coming back in the morning. There was puke in the driveway, broken glass on the ground, stains on the carpet, there was even spaghetti on the ceiling. I don't know why but there was spaghetti stuck to the ceiling. We cleaned up and had the place looking flawless by morning. I think we actually told my Mom about it years later.

Realistically, that night should have (and could have) been my introduction to bad habits I eventually picked up later down the road: smoking, drinking, experimenting with substances. But it wasn't, because I was kind of timid and skateboarding was more important at the time. One thing I did pick up that night was a heightened passion for music. One of the kids at the party threw in a tape as I was leaving the room that made me stop, turn around and ask what we were listening to. You know when you hear a song that makes you freeze up? Stop everything you're doing and go on a mission to find out what it is? Life can resume as soon as I find out what we're listening to. I love that. It was a group called *Channel Live*. A Hip Hop group out of New York. The production made you want to hump the speaker. This was different. It wasn't Cypress Hill or MC Hammer. I couldn't describe it but I really liked it. It was what's considered Boom Bap, a signature east coast sound but I didn't know that at the time. That album elevated my life long fandom of being a hard-core rap nerd.

I like all music, but I really like rap.

Getting back to smoking, drinking and drugs, that happened, but not till later that year. Like most kids at that time, I looked up to people, or watched one too many movies where smoking cigarettes was depicted as cool and eventually started stealing smokes from my dad. I'd light up in the backyard when nobody was home. I didn't even inhale, I didn't even realize that was involved until my sister and some of her friends showed me. Lisa was a great role model. My sister was my ace though. She didn't reject me, she always invited me along and introduced me as her little bro. If I was getting into mischief or bullshit, she figured I might as well do it with her and older folks that knew what they were doing. More so than I did anyway. I drank my first 40oz with my sis, smoked weed and did mushrooms with her for the first time, she even taught me how to shoplift and hustle folks. Lisa actually used to be a borderline clepto. We stole everything from lunch, to jackets, to shoes, to household appliances. The hustles depended on the surroundings but using Zoe often helped. She was like, nine years old at the time, crazy cute kid. We'd steal candy then give it to her to sell to folks downtown around the plaza. We made up a pitch about raising money for school blah blah blah. Worked like a charm. When in doubt, exploit your little sister for weed and beer money.

When I wasn't learning the tricks of the trade with my sister and her people, I was in the streets with my boys from school, mostly just skating. Skateboarding is an awesome way to bond with whatever city or town you're in. You learn about where you are, see a lot of weird shit, it's always an adventure. You never know what you're going to get into being in the street all day. Hanging around the popular skate spots, I inevitably met other kids hanging around the same places. Kids from different schools, kids from out of town, etc. I met some of my life long friends at these places, primarily at one spot, The Bataan Memorial Building. Today, this place is good for nothing but back in the day, it was a good spot for street skating. I owe this place for relationships I still hold dear. Off top of my head, these are people that came around about this time that deserve mention.

Reese – Reese had just moved back from Denver when we first met. He had a tremendous 'city' kind of demeanor. He was cool, sharp, friendly (if he liked you) and real popular at the time. He knew everybody and I met a lot of other folks through him. We just clicked, got on like a house on fire. We were inseparable pretty shortly after we met.

Chuck – Chuck was a kind of an asshole but he was cool, especially if you had some weed to smoke. He was a good skater, kid had great style. Really funny dude that everyone liked being around. He was all about skating, partying and eventually, DJing, before it was trendy. While the rest of us were bumping beats and lyrics, Chuck always had some

DJ mix tape on him. He loved scratching and the overall hilarity that came from the samples and quips that DJ's used. I remember when he got his first turntables.

Riff – Riff was a hard head, impossible to win an argument with. His mom was the only person I ever saw get him to admit he was wrong, which he often was. Not an amazing skater but determined. His passion was admirable in everything he did. He was what you might call over confident, but I suppose that was part of his charm. His older brother was part of the group of first generation skaters we looked up to, so Riff was an important member of the crew.

Tony – Tony was my right hand man. I basically lived at this kid's house. He was a great artist, skater and a rap music aficionado. I always wanted to get my hands on what Tony was bumping. He was the dude that had the new joints before they came out, if you were lucky he'd dub you a tape. He was low-key and stuck to our circle or himself. He always strived to be kind of different and just do his own thing.

Clark – Clark and I both had European parents. Came from good upbringing but were into all the same scandalous shit with all the same people. He was smart, generous, and threw the best new years parties Santa Fe has ever known (with some help from his brother). This dude is hilarious. I still have inside jokes with him from when we were kids. I was a groomsman in his wedding.

Joe – Joe moved to Los Angeles from Santa Fe in high school but he kept in touch and made occasional visits home. He originally pursued acting but found his true calling in music production. I co-produced my first instrumental with him on Alto Street at the boys and girls club. To say Joe is charismatic would be an understatement.

Donny – Donny and Joe were like Tweedledee and Tweedledum back in the day. He also went to L.A to pursue acting but eventually turned to music. This guy's a riot, Donny so much as breathes and it's entertaining. He hosts parties as well as performs and records music with artists all over the world.

Jean – Jean is one of my oldest girlfriends. She was a 'girly' girl but still managed to be one of the guys back then. She's smart, talented, well traveled, the works. This girl doesn't half step; she puts her heart into everything she does.

Amy – Amy is my other veteran girlfriend, she and Jean were friends but Amy was cut from a different cloth. She was tough, had an older brother, that story. She was sharp as nails but still managed to be a troublemaker when we were kids. She wasn't 'girly' but didn't lack femininity. This girl is strong, a force to be reckoned with.

There were plenty of other people around during this time that are worthy of mention but off top, these people share some of my fondest childhood memories. A little while after we made the Bataan and various other locations our home away from home, Santa Fe wised up and built a skate park. We were constantly getting kicked out of places for skating there, so the city finally established a place for kids to go skate and stop bothering city officials and business owners.

It kills me sometimes, how people die.

—Markus Zusak

4

The park was garbage in comparison to most but it was all we had and we were happy to have it. The skate park became the center of the damn universe for Santa Fe youth. It wasn't just skateboarders or kids on bikes and rollerblades. Everybody hung out there, everybody. You need a sack of weed? Go to the park. You need any other drugs while you're at it? Go to the park. You're looking for a party? Go to the park. You're looking for so and so? They're probably at the park. Which was helpful considering we didn't have cell phones back then. You never knew how the day was going to end at the park. There were fights, accidents, all kinds of drama and weirdness. Not so much with us, we were usually bystanders. But man, I remember seeing a lot of strange shit go down there. One episode that stands out was when a dude got stabbed with a butter knife during a big brawl. Followed by a ridiculous attempt by some idiot to steal a cop car and run it into a street lamp. When we weren't skating or ducking and dodging nonsense, we were throwing water balloons at unsuspecting vehicles and tourist busses across the arroyo that separated the park from a main road. Occasionally someone would turn around and come after us, then we'd have to run.

About a year or so after my family and I moved into town, we moved again. We moved a lot. We were still in town but on a different side, nice hood, nice place, although smaller than the last. I'm thirteen and the parents are back at it full time. It seemed like they were fighting almost every night for a while there. Which was funny because around this time, it came to our attention that our folks smoked weed. Lisa and I were excited. We could smoke in the house and didn't have to keep it a secret. My parents were down to smoke with us as long as we kept it on the hush. We tried to ensure that mom and dad were high all the time after that to keep the drama to a minimum. It worked sometimes.

A little later down the road, mom and dad threw in the towel. After twenty years of marriage, they finally agreed to divorce. I was actually relieved when they told us. It was time, they weren't happy and it was making everything at home suck. Dad was having difficulty with some kind of legalities pertaining to his citizenship and could no longer practice law in the U.S. He had been giving seminars as opposed to being in court and he wrote a couple of books along the way. Pretty sure I mentioned that earlier. Anyways, when it was all said and done, dad decided it would be best to go back to England. I didn't mind my folks divorcing but I wasn't expecting my pops to bail halfway across the globe. It didn't happen immediately but not too long after they split, dad made tracks. This was a sad time, life threw a curveball and I was having difficulty adjusting. They say life is what happens when you're making other plans, or focusing on something else.

Ain't that the truth, I was barely a teenager (puberty), was starting middle school, the folks were splitting, dad was leaving. Then, my friend Daniel died.

Daniel was my first up close and personal experience with death, I met him through Lisa at the skate park, we used to throw water balloons at tourist busses together. I smoked weed for the first time with Daniel. I even remember what he was wearing. Lisa broke the news to me, sobbing. She was devastated. He was on a school trip somewhere around Abiquiu Lake. He jumped off one of the cliffs into too shallow of water and cracked his back or maybe hit his head. Either way, he drowned. He was 15-16. I tripped out; I cried and endured all the other glorious emotions that come with being on the receiving end of that news. But shock is what really got me. Trying to envision one of your friends dying is shitty for a kid. But that's all you have, this awful story about this tragic turn of events and your imagination does the rest. I didn't have to go through it alone though, which was helpful. Daniel was popular; friend to many, we all knew and liked him. His service was packed. I wish I could say I didn't go on to become more familiar with this scenario.

When the smoke cleared, I was attending Capshaw Middle School with Tony, Clark, Donny and some other folks. Clark and I went to an 'alternative' middle school for a minute too but that's barely worth mentioning. We didn't do anything there except get high. None of this really matters because it was short lived. I didn't stick around

Santa Fe long after starting middle school because we moved to Albuquerque. Dad came with us but he was also staying with friends while preparing to make the move back to England. Mom had some kind of potential job opportunity lined up down there and cost of living in Albuquerque was cheaper than Santa Fe.

If you've never been to Albuquerque, allow me to give you a brief but descriptive breakdown. It's ugly, there's nothing aesthetically pleasing about this place. They have serious issues with car theft, drugs and gangs. The number of head shops, church's and tattoo parlors is offensive. The show, *Cops* was once banned from filming in Albuquerque because they shot there so much, the mayor was concerned it would start to affect tourism. There's an area of town called *The War Zone*. It's not just a street thing either, government officials have referred to this geographic location by that title. Plus it's basically a breeding ground for cockroaches. So yeah, let's move there.

We rented a house on Tracy Street in the northeast heights, which sounds a little nicer than it actually was. It wasn't far from my new school, Hoover Middle School. Hoover was like Turquoise Trail but with more white people. The white kids were mostly skaters, jocks and Goth/Metal weirdos and only ran with their own scene. The brown kids were mostly gangstered out and they naturally kept to their own, although they liked fucking with everyone. I did surprisingly well here; I was seasoned to the New Mexico public school dynamic and had a better handle on it. At this point I'm a full-blown pot-head so while I'm dipping in and out of classes, mingling with the new breed, I'm ultimately looking for a weed hook up. That and someone to just smoke with.

My folks were relying on me at this point to find a new connect for them too. The skater kids weren't quite there yet, the jocks only drank (which I wasn't opposed to). The metal kids were all tripping on acid and the nerds and bookworms were obviously useless. But the cholo kids! Those guys were smokin'. I would overhear them talking about it in the hall in between classes so I started thinking of a way I could approach one of them without getting my money jacked. Turned out I didn't have to because shortly after, one of them actually approached me. I was walking home from school one day and crossed paths with a familiar face.

His name was Ray; he lived at the bottom of my street. He was smoking a cigarette in his front yard and as I walked by (purposely not making eye contact) he whistles at me and says, "Hey white boy, you need some weed?" I turned around and asked him if he in fact lived there. He said, "Yeah, what the fuck does that matter?!" I said it didn't but if that was the case, I didn't live far and could go grab some money from the house and be back soon. I asked to see some product before leaving. He had it, the price was right, mission accomplished. I found my weed hookup, and he lived down the street. I copped a sack and blazed a couple bowls with him for selling it to me.

Ray was cool, he could smoke. Most kids at that age take a couple hits and they're blitzed, as they probably should be. Ray had been smoking longer than me, he supposedly started when he was nine or ten years old. When little kids smoke together, it's like a bonding ritual, at least it used to be. There was a procedure involved, kids today will never experience the sense of accomplishment attached to deseeding a twenty-dollar sack of dirt weed. I had made an unexpected friend who also happened to be a neighbor. Ray's a memorable person at this point in my life for other reasons as well. His brothers were car enthusiasts and they built and fixed up show cars, primarily lowriders.

I remember hanging out in his front yard watching them paint and assemble these fly gangster rides. Their mom would make these delicious tamales and always asked if I wanted to stay for dinner. She was a sweet lady. Ray put me on some hood shit, he got me into Bone Thugs n Harmony, Master P, stuff like that. I put him on Channel Live and less gangster style rap that he wasn't paying attention to but might have liked. I liked spending time at Ray's house, there was always weed to smoke and good food to eat. He introduced me to a world I'd always felt shunned by. He got me in with the other vato kids at school too. Always having a bag of weed on me helped.

I made good with the jocks and other kids on my own and in the event that there were problems between anybody, I was usually the one breaking it up. When it came down to it, I felt more connected to my cholo buddies, so I started dressing a little more like them. I rocked jerseys, slicked my hair back, you know, tried to have an identity. That shit's important in junior high. But I still had my skateboard, which confused people. I remember one time a kid flat out asked me, "So are you a gangster or a skater?" Because you obviously couldn't be both, right? Sorry pal, I guess I'm a gangster skater? I didn't really know, I was just doing what felt comfortable or looked dope.

I didn't only run with the gangster kids. I had my three amigos, Darren, Billy, and Casey. Casey was a skater, Billy rode stunt bikes, did BMX competitions, shit like that. And Darren was just a maniac. Darren lived in between me and Ray, so we spent a lot of time together. He was mature for his age, one of the few kids I knew back then that wasn't a virgin. He was originally from Utah; his family was Mormon. I think they moved to Albuquerque from Arizona. He was funny, usually in a good mood, the kind of dude that could pick up your mood just being around him. Always down for whatever, that whole Mormon rebellious thing I guess. His family eventually moved and I lost touch with him. Casey came from nothing but was a high-spirited kid. He was always down for skating, partying and chilling with girls. He eventually joined the military, I'm sure he made a good soldier. Billy had a great sense of humor, chicks loved him, he always had a girlfriend.

I can't remember where he was originally from. He skated a little bit but bikes were his passion. Which brings me to a story – Billy lived up the way from me and you could take a short cut through a ditch to get to his apartment complex. I was at his house one day when we ran out of smoke and I asked him if I could use his bike to run back to my house real quick to grab more. That was like asking to bang his girlfriend. His bike was his pride and joy and he didn't let anybody ride it, never mind actually take it somewhere. I was persuasive and he eventually gave in. I wouldn't be gone long. I could've walked but riding the bike would cut the time in half. I went to my house, grabbed the bag and was in route back in no time.

On my way back up the ditch, I saw a kid up the way walking towards me, he was bigger than me but was young and didn't look threatening. He stopped me when I went to pass by him. He asked if I had a lighter, I said, sure. He whips out a bag and a pipe and asks if I want to smoke. I say, sure! I park the bike, we copp a seat, blaze, start talking, it's all good. He eventually turns his attention to the bike, starts asking about it, says he used to race. I tell him it's my friends, he races too etc. he asks if he can hit a couple licks on the ditch. I say, go ahead. He gets on the bike, hits some jumps, pops some this and that and right when he appears to be finishing up, he makes a sharp turn. He bails down the ditch like lightning after gaining speed from the sides. Running after him would have been asinine. I stared in disbelief while I thought to myself, he's fucking with me, he'll be back. I sat there for a few and waited. He never came back. I walked back to Billy's house thinking about how I was going to explain to my boy that I got his pride and joy stolen from right under my nose. It was bad. He freaked, his mom yelled at me, he didn't speak to me for a while.

I was mad. Mad at myself and mad at that ditch. I didn't step foot in there for some time after that but Billy eventually forgave me and I eventually forgave the ditch. As time passed, I started using it as my short cut again and not too long after our reconciliation, that ditch actually changed my life.

Graffiti is beautiful, like a brick in the face of a cop.

—Hunter S. Thompson

5

I'm fourteen, it's 1998, I'm in 8th grade. Which is cool because in middle school, 8th grade is top of the food chain. My only problem back then was being in the principal's office regularly. Mostly for talking back to teachers, attendance or dress code. I was always in violation of dress code. The code was initially meant to provide a solution to gang issues or just make kids feel safe in general. Basically, nothing that could be viewed as gang related. No baggy clothes or sagging pants, no sideways hats, you couldn't wear certain shoes, etc. Obviously I refused to conform to this nonsense. Identity, remember? I'm a skater *and* a gangster. My pants are sagging fool! I took the punishments, I took the detentions, I think I took potential expulsion. My mom tried to buy me pants that 'fit' for the sake of the principal's sanity but I wouldn't wear them. She didn't care that much at the end of the day. She thought the whole thing was pretty dumb. In a school of 800+ kids, I was one of the few the whole office knew on a first name basis.

I was denied a field trip to wherever the fuck, due to all my strikes, if you will. You had to uphold certain grades and behave your damn self in order to partake in the fun stuff. I blew that several times. Which was actually cool because when the class went on a trip you were exiled from, you got to go home early! It was like a half day, I had no qualms with the situation. So here I am, walking home early one day and I run into my man, Adrian. Adrian was one of the homies who was also usually in some kind of trouble. He had been banned from the field trip as well and was actually walking to Ray's house. Along the way he suggested dipping into the ditch so we could puff while we walked. I hadn't strolled the ditch in sometime but I was with it and naturally felt more comfortable having Adrian with me.

Adrian was about my size but had all kinds of crazy cousins that weren't to be fucked with, all those kids did. There was a split in the ditch where if you went right, you'd come up on the bottom of my street where Ray's house was. If you kept going straight, you'd end up pretty much at my back yard. So when Adrian split to Ray's crib, I just kept on to go home. I was stoned and thinking about everything that took place over the last few weeks. My head was down, my feet were dragging. I thought about Billy's bike getting jacked and if I would ever see that asshole again. I took my eyes off the ground at that point, figured keep my head up, maybe look ahead. That way if anyone's coming, I'll see them. I didn't see anyone but I did see something. It was further up ahead on the side of the ditch; I couldn't quite make out what it was. It wasn't an animal or an object, or a dead homeless dude. It was bright, it was vibrant, it was huge, it was colors. It was words.

I had seen graffiti before but this was different. It wasn't the usual SUR 13 or WSL or 666. It was crazy, it was beautiful with a really urban feel to it. It was funky, it was fresh! It looked like a mural the city had granted permission (which they hadn't, it was illegally placed there). More importantly, it was legible. It didn't make any sense to me but I could read it, it said DESK GREY. Graffiti had sparked my curiosity before but this shit kind of blew my mind. I zoned out on it for a while before continuing on my way home. I had questions. I was intrigued by who did it, why they did it, when did they do it, what did it mean?

When I got home I went to my room, busted out a notebook and started trying to imitate what I had seen on the wall. I grabbed a camera before heading out to school the next morning so I could take a picture of it on my way home. But by the time I got back there, to my shock and disappointment, it was gone! There was just a big gray square of what appeared to be freshly coated wall where this masterpiece was not even twenty four hours prior. What the fuck?! I was pissed. I even questioned for a minute if I imagined the whole thing. I never looked at graffiti the same way after that. Whether it was some chicken scratch crack-head scribble, a gangbanger marking territory, or someone who appeared to have some talent, I studied it all.

Turns out that the message on the wall that day wasn't actually a message. DESK GREY were names, two guys, DESK and GREY. The more I looked around, the clearer it became that most of the writing on the wall was just that, an alias. People leaving a mark or a story like 'Kilroy was here' or 'Cornbread'. When it came down to it, most 'taggers' or 'writers' were basically just letting you know they exist. I was into it; I chose my first name and began attempting to make my contribution. I wrote SKETCH, which wasn't an awful name but wasn't great. Not terrible for a rookie.

There was a time when I probably could've filled the remainder of this book talking about graffiti so before we move forward, let's cover some basics about this brilliant and nonsensical underworld. Graffiti is challenging as fuck. Most graffiti writers are really smart, really stupid, really weird or really angry people. Graffiti is considered one of the four elements of Hip Hop, although the subculture also stems from Punk Rock. Graffiti is illegal, so that talentless asshole putting his garbage up all over town is getting more props than your homie sitting at home, doing pretty pieces in his black book. According to the unwritten laws of graffiti, (there are actually rules to this) churches and houses are off limits. So if you see someone leaving their mark on a place of worship or private property, they're doing it wrong. Personally, I appreciate 'wild style' piecing but was always more attracted to throw ups, straight letters and hand styles (please Google if you're not following). Coming up, I was inspired by DESK, GREY, DREAM (R.I.P.), TWIST, GKAE, MQ, TIE (R.I.P.) REVS, COST, SENTO, BATES, ESPO, ISUE, AROE77, SIZE, YEAR (New Mexico), CAN2, MBER and way too many others to mention but you get the idea. Like skateboarding, I met a lot of folks and made a lot of friends through graffiti over the years. I've seen some crazy shit and wound up in some strange situations as a result of it. I went to jail for the first time because of graffiti. I've seen it kill relationships and almost ruin people's lives, seriously.

Okay, we can get back to this nonsense later, but an introduction was necessary.

Let's talk about girls. Junior high is when you really start trying to get it in, you know? At least for most people, if you were doing more than making out in elementary, I applaud you. I've always been fascinated by women, probably because I was never really schooled on how to pull them. My dad just basically assured me that sex was cool and if I had the chance, I should do that shit. Although he made a point of saying "keep it in your pants until you're at least sixteen." Which I did, I didn't actually lose my virginity until I was seventeen. Mom wasn't going to talk to me about all that so I was trying to figure it out for myself from day one. Fortunately for me, I'm not hideous. Actually I might be now, but back then my looks usually broke some ice for me. I almost never tried to talk to a girl unless their friend or another reliable source had confirmed that she thought I was attractive first. Girls always liked me, I never really had problems but I could have done better. Once I got the green light that I wasn't ugly, I felt more confident trying to holler, like I wasn't starting from zero. I 'dated' several girls at

Hoover but the ones that are especially memorable are Alyssa, Carmen and Ava.

Alyssa was hot, like, really hot. She was quiet and socially awkward but really cool to hang out with when nobody else was around. It took almost nothing to get this girl's clothes off. She was almost aggressive to the point that it made you feel insecure, like she'd been around the block already (I think she had been). I never sealed the deal, lord knows I could have but I was a puss. I settled for my first blowjob. In the Too Short song, *I'm a player*, he says, "I was only fourteen when I first got my dick sucked, now I'm grown up and I really like to bust nuts." I'd like to think this is one of several things Too Short and I have in common. I hung out with Alyssa for a little while until I met Carmen, who turned out to be her neighbor. I totally didn't do that on purpose. It was okay because Alyssa actually started dating one of my friends not long after anyways. Kids are grand.

Carmen was crazy; she was Italian and had a serious attitude. She was the kind of girl that would fight a dude but at the same time was capable of being very lady-like. I brushed up on my romance skills with her. She was really into kissing, holding hands, nibbling ears, biting your neck, shit like that. It turned out that she had actually dated Ray in the past. He laughed when I told him I was hooking up with her. He didn't care though. Carmen eventually got bored with me, she wanted to fuck and I was too bitch-made to go through with it. I was crazy nervous and intimidated though. This was before pornification took over the world. Anything I knew about sex, basically came from a magazine. I thought it would be cool to have sex for the first time with another first timer. Yes, if I could go back and slap myself, I would.

Shortly after that epic fail, I started dating Ava. Nothing really significant went down with me and Ava at the time but I did actually lose my virginity to her a few years later. Ava was fine, big boobs, nice body. She was more like a skater girl. I liked Ava, she was also a virgin at the time and she always had weed to smoke. In fact, it turned out that her parents actually grew plants at their house and I bugged out the first time I went over there. They had this beautiful place that went back to what felt like an addition to the original structure. Before taking me through, she told me I couldn't tell a soul about it and that her parents could get in trouble. I swore silence and walked into what felt like some shit out of the movie, *Labyrinth*. There were weed plants everywhere, tall ones. The plants surrounded a hot tub that had melted candles all over it and there were tropical birds flying freely around the room. I'm not exaggerating. So yeah, I tried to keep her around for a while but we eventually split for whatever reason. Probably had something to do with the fact that we were all of fourteen years old.

Anyways, let's talk about Wu-Tang. My first concert, Lisa took me, just the two of us. Mom let us take her car. Looking back on a lot of these scenarios, my mom was either really cool or just kind of naïve. Either way, Wu-Tang kind of ruled my world back then and going to see them live was a big deal. It was the *Wu-Tang Forever Tour*. The show was awesome, I remember thinking how cool it was just being in the same room with all those guys.

I think around that same week, my dad came over to pick up some of his stuff and make the final preparations to leave. He and mom ended up in the kitchen, talking, drinking, smoking, like they did. Lisa and I persuaded them to let us join. We figured dad was leaving, so lets kick it. We rolled one up and poured ourselves a glass of red wine. I'd never really drank wine before but I remember thinking it was easy to drink. I threw back my glass and got another, and another, then another, and I think another. My mom cut me off but it was too late. I was gone. Never even saw it coming either. I was on the floor, assed out. Couldn't stand, couldn't walk. I was hammered. I'd been drunk before but not like this. I vomited everywhere; I remember that shit looked the same coming up as it did going down. The next day I felt awful. My first hangover. I think that was my first alcohol induced barf. It was probably more amusing than I made it sound, guess you had to be there, whatever. So, yeah after that, dad kicked rocks. I don't remember the official goodbye but I didn't see him for some time until I actually went to visit him in England.

Mom's original job opportunity wasn't all it was cranked up to be and we were contemplating moving back to Santa

Fe. Junior High was coming to an end and I was bummed about everyone separating. Most of us were fitting to go from Hoover to different high schools. Back in Santa Fe, all my friends were attending the same school. Reese, Chuck, Tony, Riff, Clark, Jean and others, they were all starting high school together. That sounded fun, I wanted in on that. The school was private though. I hadn't been to a private school in years and at this point the money wasn't there. That being said, my mom is and always has been a miracle worker. I'm not sure how but she managed to get me in on a scholarship. Reese's dad was on the board at the time so that probably helped. Either way, I got in. We moved back to Santa Fe and I started my freshman year at Desert Academy.

High school isn't a very important place. When you're going you think it's a big deal, but when it's over nobody really thinks it was great unless they're drunk.

—Stephen King

6

Desert Academy was actually an old spa and resort before being turned into a school, so the layout was weird. It was a beautiful piece of property; kind of surreal and nothing like your average architectural school plan. Most schools are designed by the same companies that design prisons. The school was on the outskirts of Santa Fe in La Cienega and I had to catch the bus out there every morning from our new digs on West San Francisco Street. Although at this point a few of my friends started driving and would occasionally give me a lift. You were actually allowed to leave campus during lunch if you were either in a certain grade or had permission to do so. Those of us that weren't allowed to leave would just hop in someone's trunk and tag along for the ride.

They eventually caught on and started checking for that though. There were rich motherfuckers attending this school so those of us that were less privileged tried to take advantage. I was always hustling kids for lunch money, weed, cigarettes, pitch-ins for parties, anything I could. Sometimes we'd get a sack of weed and flip it for more than it was worth. Other times we'd roll joints and sell them for ten dollars a pop. One time, I actually sold somebody a sack, then stole it out of their car thirty minutes later. I'm not proud of that. If we weren't playing folks or making the teacher's lives hard, we were just being punks. There was a hill at the edge of the parking lot where everyone would hang out and smoke in between classes.

There was this kid who used to get a ride to school every morning in a limousine, seriously. He was awkward, probably didn't have many friends. He would come over to the hill and attempt to bum cigarettes from us on occasion. We complied with his request under the condition that he let us roll him down the hill in a trashcan. He was down; this dude would willingly get in the trashcan and let us humiliate him for a smoke. I don't know if he was looking for some form of acceptance or just really wanted a cigarette. Maybe he was into it, maybe he had a trashcan fetish. Anyways, this is the kind of shit we were doing freshman year. We were assholes, if I could go back in time and punch fifteen year old me, I totally would.

Although I made my graffiti discovery by myself in Albuquerque, my boys all made their own back in Santa Fe around the same time. I was excited to come home and find that everyone was on the same hype because now I had people to share and do it with. Reese wrote MASH, Tony wrote DELT, Chuck wrote KODE and Riff wrote FAME. These guys were my first crew and partners in crime. Tony was good, better than the rest of us at the time. He was well rounded. He came up with the name for our first crew that we attempted to take seriously. He also gave me my first real name, which was ADDICT but I spelled it, ADIKT. The homies called me DIKT. I had tried other names after SKETCH but nothing stuck.

We eventually got more involved with the scene and inevitably started meeting other writers from Santa Fe and Albuquerque. Most of them were older than us, which was good because we were in a position to learn something. Some folks took us under the wing, others wouldn't give us the time of day but we all knew about each other.

Around this time, smoking and drinking constantly was getting dated so we started expanding our horizons. Some people started messing with pills, others were checking out hallucinogens, some folks just went straight for the harder shit. I liked mushrooms. I didn't really have any desire to tamper with hard drugs. I felt safer sticking with stuff that came from the earth. My folks always told me fucking with man made drugs was dangerous. I got down on some shrooms though. One summer, I took mushrooms almost every day. It was crazy. I eventually had a really bad trip and stopped doing them all together.

I got my first job, freshman year, working with Riff doing manual labor. We set up and took down big art shows, events and things of that nature. It didn't last long but it was a good experience.

Things at home were rough for my mom at this point. My

dad had been gone for a minute and wasn't helping out. Mom was hustling odd jobs and doing what she could to keep things afloat so I was looking for other ways to keep a little money in my own pocket. I had friends that would break me off weed to sell but I usually ended up smoking it. The rave scene in Santa Fe started really going off around this time and I knew some kids that were slanging acid and ecstasy. I'd never done any of that shit and frankly had no interest, so it made me a good candidate to sell it. I was small time, I never took anything home. I showed up now and then and helped out for the night, got paid and left, that was it. I met other writers and b-boys (break dancers) through that scene, usually from out of town, one person in particular, my friend Kurt. Kurt was originally from Southern California, cool kid, talented b-boy and a good writer, kind of dude that was always looking out for people. He was about three or four years older than me. He wrote GROUCH back then but eventually made a name for himself writing HOUR.

Reese introduced Kurt and Jean and they started dating. We all spent a lot of time together back then, we were kind of like a family. Kurt lived in Albuquerque in those days and ran with a whole other scene of writers and hooligans. Jean was crazy about the kid and wanted to be down there with him whenever time permitted. Albuquerque was more exciting in general. There was more to do, more going on, more parties, shows, etc. One night, we got a call about a party down there that was supposed to be off the chain.

I hopped in Jean's car and rolled down there with her and a mutual friend.

When we got there, the place was jumping. This party was insane. It was three floors of packed house. Before I walked in, some guy did a back flip off the roof into the bed of a truck. He walked away relatively uninjured. There were kegs, bottles, music, dancing, and a whole lot of tension in the place. I remember a couple fights broke out before we left, which wasn't uncommon for a house party in Albuquerque. There was something off about this night from the jump though.

The cops showed up as we were leaving and the whole thing got shut down. I got separated from Jean when everyone spilled out of the house. Turns out that one of the fights that broke out earlier was connected to some of Kurt's people and there was talk of rallying elsewhere to finish what got started. I didn't want anything to do with it but figured I should stick with the crowd I was with. I didn't know anybody else there.

I ended up back at some house with a bunch of riled up hoodlums talking about some shady shit. This allegedly all went deeper than this one particular night and nothing about the situation was to be taken lightly. I remember I was ordered to lie down on the floor because there was a possibility that the house was going to get shot up. I told Kurt we should bounce but he said at that point, it was safer to stay inside. I laid flat on the floor and just listened to voices from the next room. Kurt was laying next to me saying we'd be out of there soon but had to stay put for a minute, he apologized. I told him it was cool, I was nervous but I didn't honestly think anything was going to happen. I was wrong.

Not even minutes later, I heard a shot go off, it sounded close, then one more. It happened so fast, I couldn't really process the sound before hearing tires screeching off. I don't know if it was a scare tactic or if they were actually gunning for someone, but the house got hit. Either way, shots were fired and the guys inside freaked out. They started yelling and busting out guns. They all piled into cars out front, ordering certain folks to go in certain rides. One dude told me I had to get in a truck with him. I said I was in the wrong place at the wrong time and politely declined. He basically said it didn't matter and I had to roll. Kurt stepped in and explained that I wasn't going. This guy looks at me and says, "Alright, you can sit this one out but next time you have to come."

I think Jean had paged Kurt in the midst of all the madness and he had contacted her from the house. Before leaving on what appeared to be a Goddamn thug crusade, he told me she was on her way there and to wait for her. It wasn't actually too long before the posse came back around, I heard them pulling up outside. They were high strung and kind of tripping out. They all came back in the house talking about, "It was time to go and everybody had to leave." I froze up when the second to last guy came through the door, holding a shotgun, with blood all over his shirt. I thought he had been shot but he exclaimed that the blood wasn't his.

Jean showed up just after the guys did, we left and headed back to Santa Fe. I never got the full story of what happened that night but I was told that homeboy with the shotgun blew somebody's head off at close range. He did significant time for the crime and was supposedly kidnapped only months after his release. His body parts showed up in the desert not long after he disappeared. It's a morbid story but that was word on the street.

Life at home was stressful during this time. I can't recall why but mom and I were butting heads a lot. I'm sure it had something to do with the fact that I was a stupid teenager and she was a single mom trying her best. She was on edge about everything and I wasn't as supportive as I should have been. I just wanted to get faded, skateboard, write on shit and hang out with my friends. I was slipping in school and she was pissed because she worked hard to pull strings to get me in. The principal told her I was fucking up and was at risk of being expelled due to the fact that I was on scholarship.

Lisa was living with her boyfriend and his brother at this point. Mom and Lisa were having their occasional ups and downs as well and Lisa suggested me maybe coming to live with her. I liked the idea, I eventually took her up on it. I left home on good terms with my mom and still saw her pretty regularly. It seemed like it would be easier for her if I freed up the space at the house. Lisa said I had to keep up with school and not fuck around if I wanted to live with her though so I stepped up my game a bit. Once I got settled, I started working again. Lisa got me my second job at a supermarket, so I would bag groceries on days that I wasn't in school. Life was simple.

Towards the end of the school year, I got a call from my dad suggesting that I come out to England for a visit. He had enough flyer miles saved up to float the trip and said he'd help cover my ass while I was out there. He had a housesitting gig for a couple months that could accommodate me comfortably. He wanted me to come stay for the whole time he was there. He had actually suffered a stroke not too long before that drastically slowed him down and he could use a hand around the place. He was getting old and living on government assistance at that point. He couldn't do much besides write. His days of being in a courtroom were over. We took a trip to Mexico when I was a kid but besides that, I hadn't been out of the country since we moved to the states. I was into the idea. I ran it by my mom and made the arrangements to pull it off.

It took a minute but we got it together. I even managed to bring Tony with me, which was cool because I was apprehensive about spending so much time by myself in a foreign country. It sounds alright now but not as much when you're fifteen. Tony's dad got it together for him on his side. He was into the educational aspect of the whole idea and thought it would be good for him. The only problem was getting the time off school. How do you miss two months of school and still get a passing grade? Tony and I sat down with the principal and talked about how we could make it work. We were both already on thin ice and the principal basically assured us that missing that much school would be the nail in the coffin. He proposed making a project out of the trip. He said if we did certain things, went certain places and came back with a full presentation about our travels to present to the staff, we could potentially avoid expulsion.

We agreed to the deal although we weren't ecstatic about it. Fuck it, we're going to England! Naturally, the only sensible thing to do at that point was throw an awesome going away party and that's exactly what we did. The place where Lisa and I lived at the time was directly across the street from a parking lot. We had no immediate neighbors and the businesses in the area were all closed by 5 p.m. This house was perfect for throwing parties and we went on to have tons of them but I think this was the one that kind of started it all. Tony made a flyer; we all pitched in and put the word out, got a couple of kegs, the works. A lot of people showed up, it was a blast. I remember meeting people that night that I still actually keep in touch with. We're not close but they're acquaintances. I was the man that night, everybody wanted to talk to me, everybody wanted to smoke with me or do a shot with me. Everybody had questions, everybody except the one person that really caught my eye.

She was a friend of a friend. She went to a different school but knew some of the same folks. She was cool but kind of shy. She was gorgeous, kind of mysterious and had the best smile I'd ever seen. She had dyed red hair so dark, it was almost black. She moved with an elegance that made it hard to keep your eyes off of her. Her name was Tina, and I think I fell in love with her almost instantly. Actually that's an exaggeration because I don't believe in love at first sight, unless we're talking about Salma Hayek in *From Dusk till Dawn* (before she turns into a vampire). So let's say at some God forsaken point shortly after meeting Tina, I fell in love with her. I still hate her for it to this day. Just kidding, kind of.

We'll get back to that later though, let's go to England.

England is the paradise of individuality, eccentricity,
heresy, anomalies, hobbies and humors.

—George Santayana

7

I barely remember leaving NM that day, I remember the flight attendant saying that she was going to be looking out for us and if we needed anything, to let her know. We thought that was pretty lame. We're fifteen, clearly we can take care of ourselves. I don't recall our connecting flight, I don't remember what movie we watched, I don't remember what they served for dinner. I remember it was a really long flight. The airport we flew into was about an hour or so away from where we were staying with my dad in a little town called, Glastonbury. It was more like a village, really. Beautiful little place, it was so green, amazing countryside. My brother, Max, picked us up with his newborn son, Ed. Eddie was the first of my nephews and nieces, so meeting the newest member of the Evans fam was cool. I think he was barely one year old at the time. I hadn't seen Max in a while. He came to visit once back when we first moved to New Mexico. Before that, he made a quick trip to San Diego but that was about it. I never knew my brothers well. They're both 15-20 years older than me; I suppose that made it difficult to be close.

Charles and Max are both cool as fuck though. Charles followed closer to dad's footsteps, he went to law school, became a barrister (that's what they call lawyers over there). Max walked more of his own path. While Charles was probably kicking ass in school, Max was probably sneaking into concerts. They both loved music. Charles played some guitar, Max played drums, it fit his personality. I don't know if my brothers actually ever jammed together but I know they were always pretty tight, regardless of their differences. Today, Charles still practices law and I believe Max is an Arborist. I think that's the correct term, one who manages forests and treats diseased or damaged trees. So Max tracks us down at the airport, we grab our bags, get in the car and my brother whips out a big hash joint.

He said we were going to make a stop on the way to Glastonbury, I inquired but he said it was a surprise. I was excited by the new surroundings and was enjoying myself, especially after smoking that spliff. Everyone in England (and I think most of Europe) combined a little tobacco with their stash, it was the norm over there. Max was giving me the lowdown on Glastonbury, dad, and the overall situation when we started nearing our surprise destination. It turned out to be Stonehenge!

If you're not familiar with Stonehenge, It's a prehistoric monument, which happens to be one of the most famous sites in the world. Archeologists believe it was built anywhere from 3000 BC to 2000 BC but nobody is sure how. It's magical, one of the most amazing things I've ever seen in person. I knew Stonehenge was in England but I didn't know it was actually on the way to where we were heading. I was caught off guard and still super high from that spliff. We hung out, took it in, snapped pictures and continued on our way to Glastonbury. When we got there, it was like we drove through a time portal. I felt like we had arrived in a medieval setting, which was a fairly accurate way of describing it. Turns out that Glastonbury is notable for myths and legends concerning Joseph of Arimathea, the Holy Grail and King Arthur. Basically, if those guys did in fact exist, they spent some time here.

It didn't take long to drive through town and up to the house where we would be staying for the next few weeks. Like I said, Glastonbury's really small. I think the population is about 8,000. The house was a surprisingly good size, it wasn't huge but it was larger than I thought it would be. I think Tony and I both had our own rooms. Damn, that's bad that I don't remember. Tony might have actually slept in the living room; we spent most of our time in there. We arrived to find dad posted up in what appeared to be an office or a space that he had made into one. He got out of his chair to greet us. He was excited.

I immediately noticed that he was slower than I remember and he looked noticeably older than the last time I saw him. The stroke did a number on him. He had mentioned previously in letters that he had lost his ability to play the piano and paint. He still tried to draw but his hand was shaky. He thought the stroke should have realistically killed him and he was grateful to be alive. He was paying better attention to his overall health but he was still smoking and drinking. And on that note, after the initial meet and greet, Max pulled out a big bag of hash and handed it to dad before he got on his way. This was clearly premeditated since dad didn't get out of the house much. That was good for all of us. Max spoke with me briefly about the next plan to meet up in London before he left. He said his goodbyes, hit the road, and without skipping a beat, Tony, dad and I sat down and rolled one up. We talked about the flight, going to Stonehenge, the project for school and what was going on back home. Dad gave us the rundown on the house, the living arrangement, the town, and adjusting to his new way of living. One thing led to another, we got faded, it got late, we called it a night and passed out.

The next morning I hopped out of bed like a kid on Christmas. I was eager to go and explore the new surroundings. Tony was in the same mode. We got ready, grabbed our skateboards (of course we brought our skateboards) and hit the town. It didn't take more than a day to explore the areas that weren't strictly residential. Glastonbury was small but surprisingly hip. We found a good record store in town and spent a healthy portion of our first day out digging for beats. We made a couple purchases and continued on our way. We rolled around looking for spots to skate. By the end of the day, we got in with some local kids, found a hook up for smoke and even came up on a liquor store that didn't ID us, so we were pretty much set.

I couldn't find weed out there to save my life. Everyone

smoked straight hash and it was difficult to find trees for some reason. I remember one of the maybe two or three times we did manage to get it, it was more expensive too. So we smoked a lot of spliffs and hash bowls. Which was fine. Smoking with the locals out there was different than smoking in the states. Back home it was 'puff puff pass'. Over here the kids would roll a really long spliff, like three or four papers and take turns smoking on it for give or take five minutes. Everyone got one turn, so by the time it went around a circle, it was gone. We talked about all the funky differences between there and back home.

The Glastonbury kids were intrigued by us and vice versa. It was cool, we all taught each other things. When I wasn't getting faded, skating, or kicking back with dad, I was scouting the historic sights and educational crap necessary for the school report. I took notes, read books, inquired with the locals about stuff. I wanted the presentation to be strong. I felt like the principal and staff back home were doubting me and I was kind of eager to prove them wrong. Tony threw in the towel early, he decided he didn't want to deal with it and was just going to drop out when we got back. I tried to persuade him otherwise but his mind was made up, so I was on my own.

When we made our first trip to London, dad rolled with us. We caught a train from a nearby town and Charles picked us up when we got into the city. I remember the first time I saw Charles; he had a great energy about him. The dynamic between him and my dad was almost like something out of a movie, they were hilarious together. He was recently married and was excited for me to meet my new sister in law, Wanda. Wanda was gorgeous. She's Brazilian, petite, dark skinned, long black hair and has a beautiful accent. She was really sweet, warm and welcoming. She hugged me and kissed my cheek as soon as I walked in the door. We dropped our stuff, got situated and had dinner. There were decorations around the house because it was close to the holidays and we were fitting to spend Christmas at Charles' place. The next day, we went and did the same rendezvous at Max's. Max wasn't married at this point but I'm pretty sure he and my now sister-in-law, Helen, were engaged. Helen was also beautiful, smallish light skinned girl with short dark hair, very hip with a British accent. She was congenial; she hugged me and offered me a cup of tea when I arrived while Max hopped on spliff detail.

That night, Charles and my dad decided to go for a drink and thought it would be cool to attempt to get me into a bar with them. I was hesitant but I agreed to tag along, Tony decided to stay in. We ended up at a fairly sophisticated establishment; it struck me as the kind of place that an art dealer would take a client for a drink while trying to make a sale. Most of the gentlemen sitting at the bar were wearing suits. Naturally, I stood out and for a moment I feared that our master plan to get the fifteen-year-old tourist a drink would fail. The two lawyers I was with weren't stressing. We copped a seat at a booth in front of the bar like we owned the place. A fairly young guy approached the table to take our order and immediately asked to see my ID.

Without skipping a beat, Charles exclaimed that I didn't have my ID on me but it was my eighteenth birthday and demanded that I get served (legal drinking age over there was eighteen). My dad chimed in instantly as if they had already planned it out. He seemed almost insulted that the waiter would even ask for identification and ordered a round for all of us. I quickly adapted to my role in the tall tale and confirmed that whatever dad had just ordered would be satisfactory. The server turned tail and shortly returned with three beers. He wished me a happy birthday. I remember trying to explain my infatuation with graffiti to my dad and brother that night. I took a bar napkin and did some tags and simple letters to try and demonstrate, they weren't into it. We had a good old-fashioned family dispute over it. Naturally I lost, going up against two barristers. Charles got mad at me and Tony later in the trip for doing tags around his neighborhood. I thought it was kind of cool that he noticed though.

The graff scene in London was great. The city was killed so we couldn't help but want to leave a mark before heading home. We would take the underground from Charles or Max's house and head into town to skate around areas like Piccadilly Circus and various other spots. We always tried to catch a couple tags before leaving. We did Christmas with the family at Charles' house and spent New Years at Max's place. It was the millennium and everyone was freaking out about the end of the world, the computer crash and all that. We actually stayed in for that one. We got a couple bottles and just got trashed at the house. I think Max and Helen went out for a bit but Tony and I had had our fill of the city.

New Years is one of those occasions that no matter what you're doing, it's cool. Whether you're going ape shit with your friends or chilling at home with your grandma. I was content drinking, smoking and reflecting with my best friend at the time. We talked about the trip, the things we'd seen and done, the people we'd met, what we would do when we got home etc. we'd been in England for almost two months at this point. I can't describe the journey in its entirety but I hope I provided a meaningful insight because it was an important experience. Sadly, I haven't seen that side of the family since. My nephew, Ed, is grown now and Charles and Wanda went on to have two kids of their own, Sophia and Henry. Lisa made her additions to the family tree with Averie, Hazel and Cedar and Audrey is number seven by way of Zoe.

Don't be a fool, stay in school.

—Mr. T

8

The first thing that stands out about the trip home from England is my connecting flight to Albuquerque from Atlanta, Georgia. The photo on my green card wasn't up to date and the lady at customs didn't believe it was actually me. The picture was from when I was a toddler; I was two or three years old. I suppose she had a fair argument but nobody, myself included thought it would be a problem. She asked me some questions that all checked out but by the end of the conversation she was basically threatening to send me back to England. It was an ordeal, phone calls had to be made, authorities had to be contacted. I sat in the Atlanta airport wondering what I would do if I couldn't actually go home. It took a while but eventually got cleared up and I was granted legitimate access back into the country. Thankfully, it was pre 9/11.

When we got back, naturally, we threw a welcome home party for me and Tony. A lot of the same faces from the departure party attended, Tina included. I think this was the first time that I successfully wooed her. We started dating shortly after. I started preparing for my school presentation almost immediately because I knew my academic future at Desert Academy was depending on it. I had my sister and friends help me out. Kurt drew up these awesome graffiti pieces for each subject on display boards and I pasted the reports onto them along with photos and memorabilia from the trip.

When the day came to present it to the faculty, I was nervous. It was after school and I had to stay late. I greeted the entire staff as politely as I could and proceeded to attempt to convince them that I was a decent human being, deserving of a private school education. It was good, it was strong, I nailed it. I thanked everyone for their time afterwards and assured them that I wanted to be there. I was vulnerable, humble and for the first time in my life, I genuinely gave a shit about being in school. I apologized for my behavior in the past and promised that I would strive to do better.

They shook my hand and congratulated me on a job well done. They smiled in my face and made me feel like I had met their expectations. They expelled me a week later via a letter to my mom. It ultimately came down to money. One by one, they expelled everyone who wasn't paying full tuition. Except for Clark, he left on his own accord. He joined me at Santa Fe High School shortly after I was ousted. Santa Fe High was a better fit for me. It was familiar. I was back in the public school system. I already knew a lot of people there. Tina was there as well, so I was happy. Santa Fe High was a mess though. It was way too easy to skip class and get away with bullshit. It's actually turned around a bit since I left but back in the day, it was something of a free for all. We'd show up early some days just so we could smoke a blunt before first period. Then we'd go to class and just zone out or maybe even fall back asleep.

Sometimes one of my teachers, Ms. Frandina (who was actually really cool) would get mad and say, "Whoever brought the stench of marijuana into my class room, please don't do it again." Most of the kids would be looking at each other, not sure who she was referring to because it could have been anybody. We liked Ms. Frandina, but apparently not enough to refrain from getting high before her class. When we didn't have weed, we'd occasionally split a 40 oz. These days, the thought of consuming alcohol before nine o' clock in the morning makes me want to puke but in high school it was actually kind of fun to have a buzz in first period. When the security guards caught us smoking cigarettes, they would just tell us to put them out.

We ditched for lunch frequently and more often than not, just wouldn't come back. We'd go get a burrito at *Felipe's Tacos* down the way and would spend the rest of the afternoon painting in the tunnels under the street before calling it a day. I was living something of a double life during this time. Lisa and I were having parties at the house every weekend and I started falling behind in school. Kurt had moved in with us and as much as he tried to push me to succeed academically, his motivation towards graffiti overpowered everything. We were partners for a good while. Sometimes he'd insure that I had done my homework before going out late to hit spots with him but when it came down to it, getting over is what really mattered.

Lisa eventually moved on and the infamous Linda Vista party house became a thing of the past. Kurt and I decided to stick together and got our own place with a mutual friend on Cortez Street. This place was just fucking silly. It was *the* bachelor pad, a crash pad, a place for the crew to link up. The door was always open. Most days I would come home from school and there would be a gang of people hanging out, none of whom actually lived there. It was the norm, I got used to it. Coming home to music blaring, empty bottles everywhere, the house always smelled like weed. I'd partake but would eventually retreat to my room to try and keep up with school.

The parties continued on weekends and would occasionally get out of hand. Our immediate neighbors were cool though, nice Hispanic family who had chickens and they would always bring us fresh laid eggs. They had a daughter about my age; her name was Melissa. One night we had a party where a bunch of people we didn't know showed up, which wasn't uncommon. But this particular night went south after some guy tried to break into our neighbor's house through Melissa's window. He got shook and ran after Melissa discovered him. Her dad, who was really pissed, came over and let us know about it. A group of us went looking for him, we searched the whole neighborhood but to no avail.

We went back to the house and just so happened to find the kid comfortably and quite casually smoking crack on our front porch. This dude got mauled, skateboards to the face, bottles over the head, fucked up. The mob serving up street justice was going to keep beating him but I stopped them because I was worried they might kill him. They eased up but not before dragging him to our neighbor's house and presenting him to the family all bloody and beaten. Melissa's dad wasn't as into it as we thought he would be. He was grateful and recognized our neighborly efforts but told us he didn't want the culprit bleeding all over his porch. Melissa thought it was pretty cool. Her brothers and cousins approved.

The debauchery didn't let up anytime soon after that. We discovered a location where we could steal large quantities of alcohol on a fairly regular basis. A squad of guys would take turns doing runs and come back to the house with whatever they managed to get away with. My laundry room was often stacked to the ceiling with beer. We would throw parties and charge for bottles or cups. It was a good hustle at the time. We'd make a few hundred dollars a night, go back to the spot, rack more beer and do it all over again. We eventually wised up and quit while we were ahead. We were lucky to have gotten away with what we did. If we ever got caught, we'd be looking at serious jail time. The parties slowed down, which I was ok with because we lived across the street from a school and there was a lot of criminal activity going on in and around the house. If you get popped doing anything in a school zone, the consequences are automatically exacerbated.

I became skeptical about all the traffic and attention the house was getting. I decided to start working again (I left the grocery store when we moved) tried to buckle down and get through the remainder of school. It was easier said than done. My friend, Jess, was a pretty substantial support system during this time. She was older than me, had been through some crazy shit but always came out on top. Jess was smart. She used to get me out of the house and help me with my homework, buy me dinner, make sure I had weed to smoke, etc. Thanks Jess.

Our roommate, Matt, at the time was a tweeker. He loved drugs but he particularly liked speed. His fam was well off and his mom would send him money all the time for bills, food etc.

Sometimes if Kurt and I couldn't come up with our end, she would just pay our rent. I don't think she knew that most of the money she sent him, went to getting fucked up. He was a good dude, he meant well. He would buy an ounce of chronic and smoke the whole thing with us in a day, get on the phone with his mom, tell her he needed more money and take us out to dinner. So it was hard to put him in check when he was fucking up or doing shit that put the household in jeopardy. For instance, I went to a rave one night in hopes of making a little side money. I ran into Matt there and actually sold him some ecstasy.

The night went well so I ended up leaving early, treated myself to a decent dinner, met up with Kurt and went to a friend's house. When we got home at about four in the morning, the entire fucking rave was at our house. I was livid, I was asking about Matt's whereabouts but nobody even knew who he was. I pushed my way through a crowd of high, drunk and tripping people to our living room and found Matt on the couch. He was deep in a ketamine hole, he was drooling and for some reason, had a loaded shotgun on his lap. There was a five-foot nitrous tank next to the couch that he had apparently purchased back at the rave and people were taking turns 'fishing out' on my living room floor. I removed the shotgun from Matt's lap. We decided we'd inquire about it the next day. I went and stashed it in his room and kicked everyone out in a very friendly, calm fashion. We actually used the nitrous tank to our advantage and charged people to come over and do balloons over the course of the next week until it was empty. Matt didn't even remember where he got the shotgun from but he was pretty sure he purchased it from someone that same night.

Shortly after that incident, some girl's car got stolen out of my driveway. She was hooking up with Kurt at the time. We had some friends over, nothing crazy but a couple of our Albuquerque goons were visiting for the night. They noticed that she left her keys on the kitchen table after retiring to Kurt's room and decided it would be a good idea to drive her car to California. I was actually doing homework while listening to them concoct this genius plan in between aggressive snorts of cocaine. I tried to shut it down. I told them to crack a beer and chill the fuck out but they just invited me along. If it was anyone else, I would have laughed it off and gone about my business but these guys were knuckleheads. They came from broken homes, went to jail every other month, didn't have jobs or anything to lose. One of them had recently attempted to slit his own throat in our house during a drunken outburst not long before. They were part of my graffiti crew at the time, good guys when it came down to it. They looked out for me. Everybody in that crew did because I was younger and smaller than the rest of them.

That being said, they were derelicts. They weren't about to listen to a youngster try to convince them that what they were fitting to do was stupid. They told me to keep my mouth shut, come up with a creative story to tell the victim or just play dumb. Five minutes later they were gone and I was an accessory to car theft. I got myself a beer, lit a cigarette and went back to doing my homework. I decided to play stupid. When it came time for an explanation, I, along with the rest of the household stated that I didn't know them and didn't even realize there was a car in the driveway the night before. She filed a police report and they eventually located her car a couple of weeks later in the Bay Area. I eventually crossed paths with those guys again a few months down the road back in Albuquerque. I didn't even ask but I was glad to see that they were alive and not locked up.

Regardless of my efforts to keep up with school, all the bullshit eventually caught up with me. I'd just turned seventeen and was a few months into my junior year when it was brought to my attention that I was going to have to repeat a grade. I had missed too much class; the principal said I could choose to repeat the eleventh or twelfth grade. I offered to clean up my act, said I would take extra credit, make up every assignment I had missed, do summer school, anything I could. He assured me that the damage was done and even if I successfully executed my plan, I would still be held back. I had never flunked a grade in my life and I wasn't about to start now, so I dropped out. I didn't want to but I would have rather died than stayed at Santa Fe High for an extra year. Especially when I was so close to being done. All my friends would be gone; I couldn't wrap my mind around it.

When you drop out of school as a minor, you have to get permission to do so. I had to go around to all of my classes and get my teachers to sign a legal document confirming that I was being permanently released from school. Most of them signed off on it and just looked at me like I was another loser that they knew wouldn't make it but Ms. Frandina cried. She begged me to stay, told me she would help me, tried to convince me that I was making a mistake. That was hard. I told her I was sorry and to please not take it personally. I told her she was cool and I enjoyed having her as a teacher. She was really sad to see me go, until a few weeks later when several other kids dropped out right behind me. She thought that I spawned some kind of trend and was supposedly pretty mad about it. I can only chalk that up to bad timing, I don't think anybody dropped out of school because I did.

Clark and I decided to drop out at the same time, but he did it for his own reasons. We actually walked off campus for the last time together. It was the middle of the day right around lunch. He was so excited to leave. He lit up a cigarette in front of everybody, including a security guard. He asked me what I wanted to do.

I suggested going down the street to *Felipe's* to get a taco. We walked through the school gates as students of the institution for the last time. Before we crossed the street, Clark turned around and said, "Look dude, look at this place, we never have to come back to this shit hole ever again."

Painting is self-discovery. Every good artist paints what he is.

—Jackson Pollock

9

My mom was bummed, she was torn because she understood me not wanting to stay back in school but she didn't support my decision to drop out. Everybody was sort of disappointed in me, Tina included. I realize that I haven't shed any light on my relationship with Tina so far but I suppose that's because it wasn't as momentous as other events that were taking place during the same time period. I held on to my vision from junior high of the fairy tale relationship where everything could be perfect. Tina and I would lose our virginity to one another in some romantic setting and be the coolest couple ever. But that didn't happen. We were young, insecure, and just couldn't pull it together to achieve the 'mature' relationship that all of our friends appeared to be having. I was envious of that and I know she was too. We failed to understand each other. We didn't have enough in common and I gradually convinced myself that no matter what I did, I would never really make her happy. I still tried though, I was hopeful, I loved her so much. I didn't want anybody else; I refused to accept that our relationship was just a series of arguments and small talk, holding hands, making out and mediocre dinner dates.

I learned early on that it's possible to fall in love with the wrong person.

By the time Tina and I called it quits, I was jaded, heart broken and still a virgin. This wasn't cool. I was the last one in my immediate group of my friends. I couldn't partake in conversations with my boys when they would swap stories about their sexual conquests. They all made fun of me and would say shit like "Kit's scared to get his dick wet." I was pissed, my virginity had officially become a burden. I just wanted to be rid of it. The sex gods must have heard my cry because not too long after solidifying that decision, I ran into Ava at a fiesta party in Santa Fe. I hadn't seen her since middle school in Albuquerque and she was really happy to see me. A rumor started up some time back that I died and she actually thought I was dead!

For the rest of the night she couldn't keep her hands off me. She kept saying how good it was to see me. She still looked good. We reminisced about Albuquerque and talked about our high school experience. What happened to so and so, who was doing well and who wasn't, who was having kids, moved away or went to juvenile hall. We hooked up but she had to catch a ride back to Albuquerque shortly after. We made plans to link up again soon. Chuck was actually hooking up with one of her friends that she came with so we decided to take a trip down south together to pick up where we left off. Chuck's sister lived down there and was out of town for a weekend, so we invited the girls over to party with us at her place. It was a blast, we drank good beer, smoked good weed and by the end of the night, I was no longer the butt of virgin jokes.

I figured it would be a disaster but I was past the point of caring. It went surprisingly well though. She actually got off before I did. It lasted longer than I was made to believe it would. I thought I was some kind of natural. The next night I went for round two, turns out I wasn't a natural after all. Beginner's luck I guess. I didn't actually see Ava much after that weekend. We hung out occasionally, had some good times but eventually lost touch again. I went on to pretty much just being a whore because I felt like I had to make up for lost time but I'm not going to turn this into some kind of red shoe diary. Although that would be more entertaining to write about than going back to school, which is what I did.

I mostly did it for my mom. She asked if I would give it one more shot before officially calling it quits so I enrolled in a bullshit program at a bullshit institution called the Career Academy. It was basically the armpit of the Santa Fe public school system. It was designed for kids that were 'at risk' or incapable. Everybody there was pregnant, in some kind of trouble with the law, or trying to get through school faster than the conventional way would allow. The courses were all on computers and the teachers were only there incase we had questions. I remember one of them would show up to class late, reeking of booze and would just sit at her desk in total silence staring off into space.

She never spoke unless spoken to. I gave it a couple of months until I was called into the principal's office and accused of selling weed on campus.

I told him he had been misinformed, which he had been. I never sold shit to anyone at that school. He said he had the right to search my backpack as a result. I told him to fuck off but he threatened to call the police and told me if I didn't have anything to hide, there shouldn't be a problem. He searched my bag, which had several cans of spray paint in it at the time. I was planning on hitting a spot on my way home because I was taking night classes. He started questioning me about graffiti and accusing me of being a vandal. I told him to fuck off for a second time, grabbed my bag and left. I never went back. I told my mom I was genuinely sorry but I just couldn't do it. I went and got my G.E.D shortly after with Donny at the Community College in Santa Fe. I had been working full time at a restaurant, bussing tables and although I liked the owners, I didn't like the job and I didn't like the clientele. Except for Robert Englund, the guy that played Freddy Krueger. He used to come in once and a while, he was cool. I hopped around several other establishments doing similar tasks. I did it all from back of house to room service. The money wasn't awful but it wasn't great.

The rave scene had mellowed out and even if it hadn't, I didn't want to go back to that grind, even as a side-hustle. I didn't like the music and the overall scene and vibe just wasn't my style. The cops had caught on that money was being made at those events and word on the street is that there were narcs rolling the venues now.

I was never great at dealing drugs in the first place and had actually put the idea behind me until I linked up with my friend Zack. Zack was a dope dealer and all around criminal. If it made money, he was into it. I had known Zack for some time but never associated with him on a business level. He looked out for me and threw me money when I was broke, which was pretty often so eventually he offered me a small setup running cocaine for him. I didn't like cocaine, (still don't) had never done cocaine (still haven't). But again, that made me a good candidate to sell. I started riding a bike around town during the day with a few grams in my sock and usually only dealt with people I knew. I would make enough for the basic luxuries - food, cigarettes, a bottle of something, new music once and a while, maybe some gear. He told me if I wanted to step it up, I could ditch the bicycle and start riding shotgun with him on the bigger deals after dark.

I went along a few times but I had to carry a gun and interact with a lot of shady folks. I didn't like any of that; I told Zack it wasn't for me. He was cool, said he understood and it wasn't a problem. He offered to let me do runs for him if and when I needed the money but never asked me to do dirt for him again. Zack's lifestyle eventually caught up with him. He went down some years later for a list of things and served a few years at the New Mexico

State Penn. He called me fairly often and we wrote each other letters while he was inside.

After officially deciding that I wasn't a drug dealer, I buckled down and just embraced being employed. I didn't have another source of income outside of my restaurant jobs for a little while. The opportunities still presented themselves occasionally but I stuck to my decision to make money legally. No stress, no drama, no guilt, no guns, no trouble, it was worth it. I still thought about ways to make legitimate money on the side without having to work as much but I could never come up with anything worth a damn, until I sold my first painting.

I started to take painting somewhat seriously when I was about seventeen. I had been so passionately involved in graffiti and street art for the last couple of years, I barely even acknowledged other art forms. Graffiti was the only thing that truly interested me. I collected books and magazines, watched documentaries and interviews with other writers from renowned crews all over the world. You could listen to their stories while they shared their photo albums and gave you a glimpse of their studio. Most of them were showing in galleries or even museums, I thought that was awesome. It's the Batman approach: prestigious artist by day, ruthless vandal by night.

I was inspired all over again. I started buying (well, mostly stealing) paints and brushes and canvas, I would save my scrap cans and dying markers. I began looking at other materials and surfaces that could be utilized for creative purposes. I had always been artistic but now I wanted to be an artist. I had never been too attracted to drawing and more often than not, didn't have the patience for it. I was always more intrigued by abstract art or simple, affective pieces. So I started throwing paint around.

It was fun in the same way graffiti was, it was therapeutic in the same way graffiti was. If you can't comprehend how graffiti could be therapeutic, you should go vandalize something the next time you're upset. Seriously, go write whatever the fuck you want on something that doesn't belong to you, preferably a corporation or something, it feels great. In addition to really enjoying myself, the feedback my paintings received was good. People loved my work, which kept me inspired and wanting to do more. I didn't have much storage room or wall space at our house on Cortez Street so I would just give my paintings away as soon as I finished them.

I moved back in with my mom temporarily because Matt finally went away to rehab and Kurt and I couldn't keep the place by ourselves. My mom didn't have much room but she encouraged me to use whatever space I could as long as I didn't get paint everywhere. Around this time, Lisa was working at a hair salon that had a modern sort of city style feel to it, which I liked. I'd go in there and meet Lisa for her lunch break or just stop in and say hi once and a while.

Over time I got to know the other employees as well as the owner, a sweet southern lady named Regina. Lisa had mentioned to Regina in passing that my paintings might look cool in the salon and urged me to show her something. I hadn't thought about actually showing my work before. Lisa along with my mom convinced me it was a good idea; I didn't really have anything to lose. I suppose I was worried about the possibility of rejection but I went through with it. I didn't have a car so I walked to the salon from my mom's house with two 16x20 canvases to show Regina and the staff. I didn't have a portfolio; I didn't even take pictures of my paintings before giving them away. I was nervous when I got there, I hadn't felt so on the spot since my oral presentation at Desert Academy. I was preparing for potentially negative feedback or at least constructive criticism, so I was relieved when it turned out that everyone really liked them.

Regina hung them both on the wall and asked if I had more. I lied and said yes. I told her I would be back with more paintings to fill the space in the next couple of days. I borrowed pieces that I had previously given away to people and promised I would give them back after the show came down. It didn't occur to me that they would be up long term. I returned to the salon later that week to hang what I had managed to track down. Regina liked everything I had brought in and told me I was free to put it up wherever there was space. I didn't really know where to start, I didn't even have a hammer on me. My sister provided the necessaries and proceeded to help me with the task. I took one of the paintings and put it up against the wall just to see what it would look like. Lisa approved it along with another gentleman who had unexpectedly entered the room when my back was turned. He said, "That's great, how much do you want for it?" I blanked for a moment. I looked at my sister, she raised her eyebrows at me and gave a head nod.

I didn't know the first thing about selling art but I had to say something so I nervously muttered that I would gladly take a burrito and a pack of smokes for it. He chuckled and replied, "How about I just give you a hundred bucks?" I didn't even get a chance to respond before he continued on with his offer. "Do you want cash or a check?" My sister quickly intervened and said that cash would be fine. I was still nervous and trying to wrap my mind around the fact that this was actually happening.

He said he would leave the piece up with a red dot next to it until I replaced it with something else. He was a stylist at the salon and told me there was no rush.

He handed me a one hundred dollar bill and said, "Thanks, I love it." I thanked him as well and went on to hang the remainder of the show while trying to keep a calm composure. I was super excited but didn't want to show it. I finished the job and said thank you to everybody there. I'll never forget how I felt walking out of there that day. The excitement, relief, and sense of accomplishment. It was the best one hundred dollars I'd ever made. I was practically skipping home. My mind was spinning out of control; I started thinking about what I was going to paint next. I stopped to get a burrito and a pack of smokes on the way home.

Being sober on a bus is like, totally different than being drunk on a bus.

—Ozzy Osbourne

10

When I was eighteen, I attempted to move out of New Mexico. I was over it, I was excited about my newfound capability to be a salable artist and I figured that was something I could take with me. Not long after becoming set on the idea of leaving, Kurt actually asked me if I wanted to move to Seattle with him. He had friends out there and said we'd have places to crash until we got jobs and got on our feet. I had never been to Seattle but I figured it was just as good a place as any. I saved up over the next couple months, quit my job, packed a bag and purchased a bus ticket. We didn't have that much money and bussing was way cheaper than flying. I remember stepping on to the bus at the Grayhound station in downtown Albuquerque. I wanted to call *Unsolved Mysteries* and let them know I had found everyone they were looking for.

By the time we were in route to L.A from Phoenix, I was stuck in between two obese, angry black women yelling at the top of their lungs about the most intimate details of their lives. They went on for hours about their boyfriends, ex boyfriends, families, jobs, etc. I tried to sleep but it was practically impossible. I remember thinking if I had a dollar for every time they said "fuck" I would have had enough money to get off the bus and catch a flight. A new seat eventually opened up and I moved.

I wound up next to a friendly middle-aged woman who wouldn't stop talking to me about her addiction to Dr. Pepper. She wasn't kidding, either. Every time I got off to smoke a cigarette, she got off to drink a Dr. Pepper. She said she drank at least a six-pack a day. I'm assuming that lady is dead now, or suffering from serious health issues. By the time we reached Los Angeles, I was tired and wanted a shower. We hopped off the bus and began the second part of our journey down to Orange County where we were going to be staying with Kurt's mom for an undetermined amount of time before continuing on to Seattle. Kurt didn't see his mom very often and she wanted to spend some time with him since he was passing through.

Kurt's mom lived in a beautiful little part of Orange County called Dana Point. It wasn't far from San Juan Capistrano, where our friend, Jace was living at the time. Jace grew up in the area and had a car. He'd pick us up almost every morning and we'd head to the beach or go steal markers and cans, check out painted tunnels, get some weed or drive up to L.A. Jace was a determined graff writer. He especially did his thing at freight yards around the Los Angeles area back then. I had recently taken a significant interest in painting freight trains because the street scene back in Santa Fe was calming down. There were spots but you had to be selective about what you chose to paint on. Graffiti thrives on decaying surfaces, old abandoned buildings, brick, wood, metal etc. We didn't have much of that back in Santa Fe but we did have a popular railroad.

What's cool about painting on freight trains is the fact that they move. You can paint a train in California and next week it might show up in New Jersey. When graffiti started blowing up in New York in the 70's and 80's, the target of choice for writers was the subway. Street bombing was cool but if you hit a spot in the street, the only people who saw it were the ones who drove or walked by it. The subway would carry an artist's name from one side of the city all the way to the other; making stops at several stations along the way. You could paint one train and be seen by thousands in a day. The same idea applies to the railroad but instead of your name crossing the city, it's crossing the entire country. Different lines went different places. The more yards you hit, the better your chances were of showing up in more locations.

I had been painting as consistently as I could back in New Mexico but the yards were small and quite a few other folks were painting them at the time. You had to be careful not to blow up the spot because it was all we had. Sometimes we rolled up in there and the only trains that were laid up had already been painted. That was always disappointing because we usually had to drive pretty far to track down something to paint.

Sometimes you'd get lucky and they would lay up train cars in town but that was rare. Hopefully that crash course in train painting will help you understand why I jumped at the chance to go paint yards in L.A. Jace had been running with a small crew of guys from the area that were hip to several yards around the city.

If you're engaging in criminal activity in a place you're not familiar with, it's a good idea to have a host, especially if you're fucking around in a train yard. Think about all the shit that goes on in train yards, there's endless opportunity for error. There are rail cops, dogs, hobos, railroad employees and of course, trains. Humongous thirty ton steel boxes that move. When a train is about to take off, it does something called 'bump'. This process consists of every boxcar in between the engine and the caboose slamming together one after another to ensure that every car is linked up properly. It happens fast, it's loud and actually pretty cool to see, like big steel dominoes.

The most sufficient way to move around a train yard is to 'hop lines', climb and hop through the very space where the car's front and back ends meet during a bump. I've heard gruesome stories about people getting caught in between lines. In addition to that visual, depending on circumstances, one of the less desirable places to hide in a yard is underneath the train. It's a last resort but if you're painting a yard that gets monitored from the air, it seems like a semi logical thing to do. Being balled up underneath a freight train, unaware of whether or not it's going to start moving is a funny feeling. You can't help but wonder if that rust and tar is the last thing you're ever going to see.

Have you ever had one of those moments where you stop and ask, what the hell am I doing with my life? Chances are you have but if you haven't, you should go sit under a potentially active freight train while trespassing and engaging in vandalism of federal property.

You might be thinking at this point that I'm an idiot, which I wouldn't necessarily argue. I guess there's a thin line between passion and plain stupidity. Sometimes you forget the extremity of risking your freedom, your job, your relationship, your health and stability, whatever you may have to lose. All for nothing more than the sake of expressing yourself I guess, leaving a mark or making a statement. To show the world something you want them to see without giving them a say in the matter because fuck them anyway. There's an element of romance to it.

We hit several yards during our stay and even managed to get pics of almost everything we painted. I had spent time in L.A previously but never got a chance to put in work out there. I had visited Donny and Joe back when they lived together in Burbank but all we did was party and go to shows. One time I actually spent an entire day at Universal Studios in Hollywood by myself, they both worked there back then. I could either take a free pass to the studios and wait for them to get off work or stay at the house all day. So I took the pass, I went on every ride and hit every show by myself. It was actually pretty awesome.

We had been in Southern California for a couple of weeks

when we decided it was time to press on up to Washington. Kurt and I both didn't want to get back on the bus so we got train tickets. The problem was, between that and the time we had spent in So Cal, we were broke. I blew all my money on food, booze, weed, gas pitch ins etc. I ended up hitting Seattle with exactly one hundred dollars to my name. It felt like it took forever to get there. I suppose the anticipation of arriving at a place can make the journey seem longer. I tried to sleep and read most of the way but made a point of spending time in the view car for train spotting and over all sight seeing. Rolling through Oregon was beautiful.

We got into Seattle at about 8-9 p.m. and had to catch a bus to where we were staying for the night. None of Kurt's folks up there had cars at the time, which sucked because I had a heavy backpack and a duffle bag. It was a trek but we arrived at our destination in one piece. When we got there we were greeted by a squad of goons on the third floor of an inner city apartment. I don't remember their real names but I remember what a few of them wrote. Everybody was already inebriated. I was offered a joint and a beer as soon as I walked in the door. We did the meet and greet, put our stuff down and maybe twenty minutes after we arrived, it was time for a liquor store run.

Everybody grabbed a marker or paint can and rallied down the stairs. We walked for a few blocks before arriving at a corner store where everybody huddled up and started talking about a heist plan. Turned out nobody had any money. The plan was simple and really stupid. One guy went in to blatantly steal a single bottle or something light, sending the one security guard running after him. The next guy goes in and starts asking the cashier to get him condoms or smokes, something locked up or behind the register. A couple other guys pretty much bum rush the place and take whatever they can while at least one other person stands post looking out for the security guard to return.

If the cashier was willing to abandon his store, he wouldn't be able to catch anybody. And if he did, he faced being potentially harmed. This was city shit; we didn't do this back home. Seeing as it was my first rodeo and I was new to the surroundings, I volunteered to stand post outside. It worked, I couldn't believe it but it went down exactly like the locals said it would. We ran a few blocks, hopped a couple fences and all linked up at a park a little ways away. It took the first guy, the fall guy, a little longer to meet up with the rest of us but he made it. I had my doubts. The security guard took off after him like a track star but this kid blazed down the street. It was hard to say if he'd get pinched or not. I think in the end we got away with an eighteen pack and a few bottles of wine.

We sat, drank and reveled in the success of maniacal achievement. We emptied the cans and bottles and decided to go for something to eat. There was the possibility that cops were scouting the area looking for us as well so it was a good idea to keep moving. We hopped another bus.

The plan was to go get burgers from a spot called Dick's, which is a Seattle staple. It's referenced in Sir Mixalot's single, *My posse's on Broadway*. On the way there, one of the guys decided he didn't want Dick's and attempted to hit a Taco Bell. This particular Taco Bell was closed with the exception of the drive through. He walked up to the window and placed an order but the cashier denied him since he wasn't in a car. He argued with the guy for a minute before accepting defeat. He whipped out his marker and did a big black drippy tag on the drive through window, yelled "fuck you" and took off. We got to Dick's, ordered burgers, hung out in the parking lot, did some people watching, threw some tags and called it a night. I was faded and tired by the time we got back to the apartment.

The couches were taken so I slept on the floor. I slept on a few floors during my time in Seattle until I went and stayed with Reese and his stepbrother, Miles. Reese had come up to Seattle just before me and Kurt, the plan was to link up and get a place together. Miles was an old friend from back in New Mexico. He was originally from Taos but moved to Albuquerque around the same time I did back in middle school. We spent a lot of time together back then. We actually wrecked his mom's car amongst other ridiculous things. So Miles put me up on a couch in his basement while I looked for a job and tried to get my shit together.

Reese was doing the same but neither one of us was making any swift progress. Kurt actually ended up going to jail shortly after we got there. I lasted about a couple months before calling my mom from a payphone and asking her if she would please front me the money for a train ticket home. I'd already borrowed money from other people to keep me afloat and I was worried that if I kept shoplifting consistently, I'd also end up in jail out there. Mom came through like she always did. She managed to get me exactly enough for a one-way Amtrak ticket from Seattle back to Albuquerque. Reese decided to come with me; he was concerned about overstaying his welcome at Miles' place with no job or independent stability in sight. Time to go back to the drawing board.

I was officially penniless and Reese had scrounged just enough to get us home. We were going to have to share everything but we weren't going to starve. The ride was relatively smooth from Seattle back to Los Angeles, although when we arrived, we had a three-hour layover at Union Station. We went outside, smoked our last cig and decided to walk around. We strolled for a few blocks before arriving at a section of the L.A. riverbed, which was home to some of the city's significant and historic graffiti. We were psyched and both just so happened to have new disposable cameras on us. So we hopped a fence and made our way down the side to the flat ground center. It smelled awful. Reese put the remainder of his cash in his sock. We both grabbed a rock, rail spike or anything that could've been used as an affective weapon if need be and walked in one direction for about thirty minutes before turning around and heading back to our starting point. We strolled the opposite way for another thirty from there until the cameras were both out of film. We got some great flicks. I still have them all in a photo album. By the time we got back to the station we only had maybe an hour left to kill. We were good, the end of the trip was in sight and Reese had about fifty bucks to get us through the next twenty-four hours or so of travel. We could get smokes, coffee and maybe even a decent ridiculously overpriced meal on the food car without having to share. Alas, when something seems too good to be true, it usually is.

While organizing our things for departure, Reese went to retrieve the money from his sock. It was gone. He checked everything and everywhere but it was nowhere to be found. He even ran back to the riverbed to check where we hopped in and out, nothing. We were so bummed but didn't really have time to even process the situation before getting back on the tracks. We talked for a minute about what to do. There weren't many options. We weren't proud of the decision we came to but we were desperate so, we lied. We lied to anyone we could. The story was that we got mugged back in Seattle before leaving. We apologized, were charming, polite, grateful, we hustled anyone that would lend us an ear. The guy in the food car hooked us up with coffee and soda, other people threw us some change or a couple bucks here and there. We were doing alright until we met a girl about our age in the smoking car. We had gone down there hoping to bum a smoke; she was the only one there at the time. We were buttering her up with our story but one of us slipped up.

I don't remember who said what but we screwed up the ending. I said we got mugged back in Seattle, Reese said we got hit in L.A, or vice versa. She looked at us sideways and asked what really happened. We apologized and told her the truth. We confessed that it sounded dumb and assumed that people would take less pity on us if we told them what really happened. She laughed; she went into her bag and pulled out a carton of smokes, some weed and a big bag of cookies. She threw us both a pack of cigs and said we could help ourselves to whatever she had. She was like an angel sent from hoodlum heaven to save our asses. Turned out she was even from Albuquerque.

We rolled a joint and took turns standing watch at the door while hitting the weed and blowing it up into the car vent. We'd have at least one cigarette burning at the same time to cover up the smell. We talked about where we had all been, how we ended up on the train, why we were heading home etc. I got super stoned, filled up on cookies, smoked another cig and returned to my seat for the night to catch some shut eye.

When I woke up we were almost home. We said our official goodbyes before parting ways. She gave me some weed and a hug before leaving. I can't remember that girl's name for the life of me but I'll never forget her.

Reese's sister was coming to pick us up at the train station in Albuquerque but she was running late. I took off down the yard to scope the trains that were laid up since we had some time to kill. I hit a tag on one of the cars and headed back to the station. I wasn't sure what my next move was going to be but it felt good to be home.

I don't like jail, they got the wrong kind of bars in there.

—Charles Bukowski

11

I moved back in with my mom for a while after returning to Santa Fe. I went back to the restaurant grind and focused all my excess energy on painting. If I wasn't painting canvas in my mom's garage, I was on the tracks with my friend and partner in crime at the time, Sean. Sean was a train-painting machine. All he did was work and paint. He occasionally took time off to chill with his girlfriend, but his mind was almost always on painting. Sean and I both worked in restaurants, usually night shifts, similar hours. So we'd link up right after work, go paint, he'd drop me off, I'd work on a canvas, crash, wake up and do it all over again. If we finished by a decent hour I'd even try and go hang with friends or a girl afterwards. It was a good time; I was making a little money and had a productive routine. Sean was a motivator, even when I didn't want to paint, he'd convince me to come out, especially in the winter. Trudging around in snow and freezing temperatures was never fun but it was usually the best time to go out. It's not hard to get frostbite on your hands from painting in cold conditions. This was around the end of 2002; it had been a good year painting wise.

We were driving literally all over the state, hitting yards

anywhere we could. There was a time when we were averaging ten plus trains a week. We set a goal to start strong in 2003 and make the year count. We would have too, if we hadn't got arrested in the first week of January. We had been painting in Albuquerque a lot, mostly with local kids that knew the yards but when we eventually got a feel on them, we started going by ourselves. It was good for a while, Sean and I were ninjas. We were paranoid and overly careful about everything. That being said, it took a strategy to take us down.

We were painting a popular lumberyard at the time with a couple legit entrances. I say legit because they were only used by people who were allowed to use them. Our entry of choice was up and through a long cement ditch that came out at the side of the yard. From there you could hop a fence and be at the back end of the lay up. If there were employees up the way, they were probably too far up the line to hear you as long as you kept a low profile and stayed out of the light.

We'd had some close calls in this yard, one time we were painting a car that ended up getting yanked unexpectedly. We hid behind the big wood stacks only feet from the rail workers linking up the car. The paint was still fresh and we could hear them talking about how they could smell it. They assumed we bailed, good thing they didn't look for us because we wouldn't have been hard to find. I had painted this yard with as many as eight people before, four guys on each side. I figured it would have been hard to get the drop on just me and Sean, but one rail worker did.

He must have spotted us from up the way when we entered the yard. Most employees in his position would have rolled on us then and there but this guy was smart. He actually let us paint, take our time, start to finish and even snap pictures with Sean's digital camera. While we were painting, he called the cops. APD showed up, he explained the situation and quietly let them in through the back entrance. The city police literally crept in the yard and hid behind the wood stacks, the same wood stacks we had used to hide from authorities in the past. They watched, waited, let us pack up and move toward our exit and then, BAM! Flashlights everywhere, "Police!" "Don't move!" I froze for a split second, partially because I wasn't entirely sure if they really were cops or other writers trying to scare us off. That kind of shit wasn't totally uncommon. It was hard to see with the lights in my face but I could just barely make out uniforms, belts and the glare of a badge.

It was time to run. We hauled ass back to the side of the yard. You could hear them right behind us yelling stereotypical cop shit like "freeze" and "don't do it." I flung myself over the fence, landed right on my face, got up and kept running. Sean was right in front of me. I remember looking ahead at the ditch thinking if we can make it there, we can lose these motherfuckers. I think Sean even voiced it.

I honestly thought for a moment that we were going to get away. Looking back, I still think we could have if there weren't more cops with dogs waiting in the ditch. It was like something out of a movie, they were wearing headgear and all kinds of crazy shit. They looked like a damn swat team. We dropped to our knees, put our hands up, and made it known that we weren't dangerous or threatening in hopes that they wouldn't release the dogs.

Naturally they did what a lot of upstanding servants of the law do to submissive unarmed citizens - they assaulted us. One of them cracked me in the back and drove my face into the ground, pressing on the back of my head with his knee. They started yelling questions at us. Who were we, what neighborhood or set were we from, what gangs did we roll with. We knew some of the people they were asking about but we played dumb. That explained the dramatic entrance. They were a gang unit hoping to bag some of Albuquerque's more notable bangers. Poor bastards nabbed a couple of white boys from Santa Fe. Our ID's backed up our story with Santa Fe addresses and when asked how we knew about the location of the yard, we said that we had just followed the train tracks.

They were pissed. They couldn't get anything out of us, nothing good anyways, nothing they wanted. They searched our bags, went through our paint and found our flare guns. We used flare guns back then because they were cheap, easily acquirable for young people and an affective weapon without being fatal. It also didn't carry the same legal consequences. The cops said we were deranged or crazy for having them but I think it was the only thing they could really use against us besides the vandalism so they ran with it. They assured us that we would be strip searched when we got booked and put us in the back of separate squad cars.

The rail worker that initially spotted us came out of hiding to talk to the cops before we left. The officer that took me in his car was actually kind of cool, he was listening to Tupac and gave me the break down about how they got in and got the drop on us. He said it looked like curtains when I fell on my face hopping the fence. He was impressed that I got up and kept running. We went downtown, I got booked and thrown in a cold, dark, concrete holding cell with about thirteen other guys. The cell could have 'comfortably' held maybe six or seven people. It was overpopulated and smelled like body odor, feet, piss and shit all at the same time. It was hard to find a spot to sit or even crouch.

Sean and I took turns making phone calls in hopes of finding someone to get us out. Bail was $300 each with a bond, which wasn't pocket change but it was doable. It was late at night and my attempts to wake anyone up failed. As I got to talking to other guys in holding, it turned out that my bail was higher than almost anyone's in there. These guys were locked up for DUI, domestic violence, grand theft auto, etc. My bail was higher than all of them, for graffiti. Sean's girlfriend eventually came and got him while we were still in holding, I wasn't as lucky.

A few hours passed, it got light out and a guard came to move me and several other guys. I was handed an orange jumpsuit, ordered to put it on, shackled to several other guys and instructed to move. I didn't know where I was going or when I'd be able to use a phone again. I was shipped off to population about twenty minutes away and was strip-searched as promised when I got there. I was given a blanket and basic toiletries, told the house rules and shoved into a pod with forty-nine other guys. I was one of two white boys in the pod; I was the youngest and smallest person in the house. There were some pretty scary looking dudes in the pod across the hall. They were throwing signs at people through the glass trying to start shit and get folks riled up. Most of the guys in my pod just gave me a strange look like I didn't belong there or I seemed out of place. Especially the O.G's, they all called me young blood.

Some of the younger guys would come off as aggressive at first until I told them what I was in for. Then they would get excited and ask if I'd heard of their homie from this set or that click. I would lie and say yes just to appease them. I tried not to speak unless spoken to but participated in card games if I was invited. It was usually poker, they played just for sport. Until breakfast or lunchtime came around, then you had to put something in if you wanted to keep playing. I lost an orange but won a cookie.

After futile attempts to get help from people in the Albuquerque area, I eventually contacted my mom. She wasn't thrilled but said she'd make the trip down from Santa Fe to get me out. It was close to lights out when my mom showed up. I was excited about not having to sleep on the metal cot they provided for me, it was just as, if not more uncomfortable than the cement floor in holding. Zoe came along for the ride and we all went out to dinner after going through the process of getting my stuff back. They didn't return my paint or my flare gun.

I took a hiatus from graffiti after that and focused more on my canvas hustle. I was still showing over at the salon and started selling more consistently. I started branching out after a little while looking for other places to show my work, mostly cafes and things of that nature. I began spending more time around people who also made the transition from graff to fine art. Most of them were older than me and had been doing it longer than I had, one person in particular, my friend James Lofton.

James had a couple nicknames but we all mostly referred to him by his last name. Lofton had always been into art, specifically painting but he dabbled with photography. He wrote graffiti in Boston back when he was attending art school but his primary focus was always on canvas and 'Junk funk'. Lofton cranked out paintings the same way train painters did freights. He really lived it; he was an artist in every sense of the word. He sold weed, smoked a pack of cigarettes a day and unfortunately had a pretty heavy addiction to pharmaceuticals. But his life basically evolved around painting.

I learned most of what I know about painting from Lofton. My man, Rick deserves credit here because he put me on some game as well. Rick and Lofton grew up together, he was an artist too and they both used some of the same techniques. If James didn't want to share a secret with me at the time, I could usually go ask Rick and he'd school me under the condition that I didn't tell anyone. I was putting everything I learned to immediate use, it showed too. My paintings were noticeably progressing which kept me motivated. I didn't go out on weekends, I wasn't interested in partying, I didn't want to do anything except paint. I spent all my tip money from work on canvas but still mostly stole my paint due to the fact that it was expensive. This was a good time but it was short lived. Not too long after I settled back into life at mom's, Kurt reappeared in New Mexico after getting released from jail back in Washington. He had a new girlfriend who he was planning on moving in with as well as a job and a house lined up, although he was in need of a couple extra roommates. He had his heart set on a particular place that his dad had just built. No credit check, no official lease, no nonsense. But family or not, he had to come up with the required amount for rent which called for extra roomies. He asked if I wanted to partake and mentioned that Jace would be coming out from California for a while to fill the other space. Regardless of what happened in Seattle, Kurt and I had a good track record and I didn't hate the idea of moving out of my mom's again. She was on her own grind and still had Zoe living with her.

The thought of living with Kurt and Jace sounded okay. I was hesitant about moving in with a couple but I figured after Linda Vista and Cortez I could handle just about any living situation. So I went for it. It went down as planned and was actually chill for a little while. We all had jobs and Kurt and I made a small studio space out of an area in the living room. He was still more into graffiti but he enjoyed throwing paint around on a canvas, he was good too. He and his girlfriend would fight once and a while but it was never anything too crazy. Unfortunately things escalated over a period of time and the shit eventually hit the fan. Jace and I were both at work when it happened.

I got off late that night and came home to squad cars and ambulances in my driveway. The cops started questioning me when I walked up. I explained to them that I lived there and asked what had happened. They told me that there had been a suicide attempt and started leaning into me about illegal paraphernalia around the house. I walked in to find blood all over my kitchen floor. Kurt and his girl had too much to drink, got into it bad, one thing led to another and Kurt slit his wrists with an X-Acto knife. He did it right in front of her while yelling that it was her fault. I guess her family had already come to get her and the paramedics took Kurt to the hospital before I got there. They said he would be submitted to the psych ward afterwards. The cops were pretty unsympathetic under the circumstances and made a point of breaking all my glass pipes before they left. I explained what had happened to Jace and Kurt's dad the next day. Jace moved back to

California shortly after the incident and Kurt's girlfriend went back to Albuquerque where she was originally from. I once again, moved back in to my mom's house.

I turned nineteen in the midst of all this chaos but the only thing I remember about that birthday is that my friend, Bart, shot himself. Shortly after that, my homegirl, Mischa, died in a car accident. It was a sad time and I was still waiting on my court date from getting arrested in January. 2003 wasn't a great year. I put my focus back into work and painting. I saved some money and got another place with Lisa. It was small but it was perfect for just the two of us. The next time I saw Kurt, he had these outstanding scars on his wrists. He eventually sleeved both of his arms with tattoos to cover them up.

During that year Lisa and I lived together, dad managed to make it over for a quick visit. He initially came to the states to give one last seminar, which he said was difficult but still doable. Dad could always talk, (it was actually pretty hard to get him to stop sometimes) so as long as all he had to do was sit there and address a room, he was okay. Lisa and I were both working but we found time to tend to the old man as much as possible. I was glad to be able to show him my paintings and where I was displaying my work.

We hadn't seen each other in four years, we kept in touch often via letters and email but he hadn't seen much of what I'd been doing. We attempted to do a collaborative piece together but he couldn't quite pull it off. His hands had gotten worse and he said they usually ached. So we spent our time doing other things like strolling around the park near our house, having the occasional smoke or drink or eating out.

The trip wasn't long, maybe a little over a week but we made it count. I spent some time with the old man every day, I didn't know that it would be the last time we'd see each other. As time went on I began to grow tired of my job and started thinking about going to art school. I wanted to leave New Mexico again but I wanted to do it right. Save some real money, maybe go visit somewhere first before sporadically hopping on a bus. Seemed like a novel concept. I liked Seattle and even thought about going back there until it was suggested to me that I might want to check out Oakland. My man, Steve was heading back there from New Mexico to finish school.

He was into audio engineering; we used to make instrumental beats together in his room. I had heard good things about the schools out that way. I had never been to the Bay Area but I liked everything I could associate it with. I told Steve to let me know when he got comfortable and planned to go visit. Time passed and I did just that. Touching down in Oakland was cool, I exited the airport and hopped a bus to Coliseum Station where I was instructed to catch a BART train to Macarthur. Steve would meet me there and we'd make our way over to Emeryville where he was living at the time.

I arrived at Macarthur Station to find Steve out front puffing on a roach. He offered me a hit, I gladly accepted. Weed was on the verge of being legal in California and nobody cared about the occasional second hand cloud at the bus stop. I was about to light a cigarette when the bus pulled up, actually it sort of romped the curb and almost took out a street pole but nobody seemed fazed by the driver's less than graceful entrance. The doors opened and a middle aged black gentleman with a mouth full of gold teeth told us all to move along because he was behind schedule. You could hear Al Greene playing on the radio.

We got to the apartment where Steve's roommates were posted up smoking weed and playing video games. Steve was staying with a couple of friends from back in New Mexico during this time, Martin and Dave. Martin had been living in the East Bay for a few years at this point and Dave had relocated back there recently to complete school at the same institution Steve was attending. I was there for a week or so. I saw the sights, checked out schools, went to a couple parties and whatnot, hopped over the Bay Bridge to San Francisco. It was a good time, I made my decision, I wanted to live in the Bay Area. I bought some gear and music, made a plan with Steve and the boys to join the household in the near future and headed back to New Mexico.

A city is where you can sign a petition, boo the chief justice, fish off a pier, get a good hamburger or a bad girl at 4 a.m. A city is where sirens make white streaks of sound in the sky and fog horns speak in dark grays. San Francisco is such a city.

—Herb Caen

12

I buckled down that summer and focused on saving money. I worked 5-6 days a week and made a point of putting away the majority of what I made every night. I was still spending and partying but I didn't lose sight of my goal. I made extra money hustling paintings outside bars and clubs around town and even started selling weed again, just a little bit to cover other expenses. I started painting trains again with Sean and the rest of our crew so if I wasn't working or drinking, I was painting on something. This was convenient because Sean's girlfriend at the time, my friend, Haley, was living next door to me with another mutual friend, Rachel. The three of them all worked together.

I had acquired a fake ID around this time but I was spending more time at home, next door, or on the train tracks. If we got finished painting early, I would still cut to the bar for last call before walking home. If I had a marker on me I would throw tags on the way. I hadn't had any real close calls with the law since Sean and I got arrested and I was readjusting to the Batman routine. I had one last scare before leaving New Mexico though. This was stupid because it was one of the rare occasions that I wasn't doing anything. I wasn't high, I wasn't drunk, I wasn't tagging, I didn't have anything on me. I was standing in my driveway smoking a cigarette, minding my own business and out of nowhere, two cop cars roll up, several guys hop out and all pull guns on me. They were yelling at me to put my hands up and walk slowly toward them.

Confused and shocked to hell, I did as I was instructed while trying to explain that they were making some kind of mistake. I got thrown on the hood while being told to shut up and accused of fitting the description of someone who was burglarizing houses in the area. One of them put his gun right to my head while another one cuffed me. I was searched, identified, and Lisa got woken up along with Haley and Rachel to verify that I did in fact live there and wasn't a burglar. I was released but not before requesting the badge number of the dude that had his gun to my head. They laughed at me and drove off.

Fast forward to my last night in town. I was buying a six-pack at Allsup's, the gas station/convenience store across the street. There was a homeless guy outside who hit me up for a beer on my way out. I said I was keeping my beer but told him he could have whatever I pulled out of my pocket at that moment. I had fives, tens and twenties. I pulled out a twenty. I told him it was his lucky night and to not spend it all on booze. He flipped out, it was funny. I drank my sixer, smoked like a hundred cigarettes and finished packing my bags. I didn't take much with me: clothes, books, a disc man, money and a one-way ticket. I was just going to start from scratch, which I did. I was nervous on the way to the airport, I was excited though. It was officially time to go back to California.

I spent my first month in the East Bay exploring my new surroundings and just kind of adjusting. I had gone out there with enough money to hang for a minute and the lease on the apartment we were living in was almost up and there was talk of moving. We looked around Oakland and Berkeley for another spot but couldn't find anything that was quite up to par with what we were looking for. One thing led to another and we decided to give San Francisco a look. This was a shot in the dark but we figured what the hell.

Sure enough, we came across a place that was practically perfect. A four bedroom, two bathroom flat, located in the inner sunset district on 9th Avenue. This is back when San Francisco was still semi affordable. The landlord was a nice little old Chinese guy named Tommy. Tommy spoke a little broken English, accepted first, last and deposit in cash and didn't do credit checks. Everything was falling into place. We had friends in the city from back in NM who had moved out there a couple years prior. Among them were Tina and her brother, Kai. I had applied to art school around this time but was actually rejected, they said my grades from high school basically sucked and I would have to do some general education credits elsewhere before being able to re apply. I was discouraged and quickly moved on from the idea of being an art major.

I started looking for a job and figured I'd just play it by ear. The household was different at this point. It was now me, Martin, my friend, Wade and Steve along with his new girlfriend who he had recently met in Oakland before the move. They both took off to Oregon shortly after we got settled, she was originally from that area.

Martin was working for a cell phone company, Wade was serving at an upscale place and I managed to land a bussing gig at a little burger joint called Darla's. It was in my neighborhood just down the way from my house, convenient for a new kid in town who didn't know his way around just yet. Darla was a nice middle-aged Asian lady who basically ran the place by herself. It was just her, the cooks and me. I had to hustle at that place and the money wasn't amazing so I started looking for a different gig after a couple months. Darla must have caught on to my sense of detachment because she actually let me go before I successfully locked down another job. This is when shit got real. I was crazy broke during this time. I had thrown down the rest of my savings on getting our place and wasn't sitting on much when I found myself unemployed. I figured it wouldn't be too hard to find another job but it turned out to be a real bitch. I was out there every day looking, interviewing, walking all over the city in dress shoes. Catching busses and trains all over the damn place. Almost two months passed and I was scrounging, didn't eat a decent meal for a while. It was Top Ramen, spaghetti, or whatever I could pull out of Steve's box of non-perishable shit that he left behind. I actually ate microwavable popcorn for three days straight at one point. That was a shitty week.

I still managed to get out and about and have a good time here and there. It didn't take much, I really just needed a 40oz, which was cheap and it was never too hard to get a homie to spot me. My man, Willie, from Albuquerque had been living in the city for a while and knew the ropes better than we did. He was a popular cat, knew a lot of people, he'd been in school out there for a couple years. So we'd occasionally venture out to his place, get faded and get into some kind of trouble. That or witness someone else's trouble. Willie lived in the Tenderloin back then at the corner of Turk and Leavenworth and there was rarely a dull moment. This area of town has been considered seedy since the Barbary Coast. You could spend a few minutes on the fire escape and see it all from transsexual prostitutes to police brutality to a good old fashioned homeless dude taking a shit, possibly with a needle in his arm.

I saw a guy get stabbed in that area a couple years later. Anyway, I didn't let being completely flat broke get in the way of trying to have a good time. I was twenty years old and determined to enjoy my new home. I couldn't afford to leave even if I wanted to. I was basically stuck so I had to make the best of it. I finally got a call back for a job that I totally didn't want but at that point I was looking into anything with an opening. The call back was from the Hard Rock Cafe at Pier 39. If you've never been to San Francisco, Fisherman's Wharf/Pier 39 is one of the busiest tourist attractions in the country. It's the boarding location for independent cruises around the bay and tours of Alcatraz as well as all kinds of other shit. I accepted a minimum wage, no tips host position, no questions asked.

My 21st birthday was right around the corner so I told them I couldn't actually start until after that. I didn't want to get stuck training for a new job the day after my birthday because I figured it was going to be a tough aftermath, it was. Reese came out to visit; we rounded up some folks and went to my first strip club in North Beach. Everybody bought me lap dances and the strippers actually let me touch them, I was slapping ass and everything. They were totally cool with it. Maybe they were hooking me up for my birthday. Maybe I just seemed harmless. I had two girls on my lap, one black, one white, some of the best tits and ass I'd ever seen. Before we left, the foxy, pleasant black girl offered to take me upstairs. Her name was Destiny. Destiny said for three hundred bucks, we could do whatever we want for a certain amount of time. I'm glad I didn't have three hundred bucks because I probably would've gone upstairs. I ended up blacking out on Jose Cuervo later that night, fell on my face, cut my forehead and still even managed to get laid by a girlfriend. A true friend is one that will sleep with you on your birthday, even if you're wasted with a wounded face.

The next day was harsh, I threw up pretty much all morning but still got out on the town and up to twin peaks to smoke a blunt with the roommates. We hit the beach later that night for a bonfire, it was a proper 21st. My scraped forehead looks pretty stupid in all the pictures. Shortly after that, I started working at the Hard Rock Cafe. To this day, I consider this possibly the worst job experience I've ever had but I'm forever grateful that the universe placed me in this corporate shit-hole because I actually met some of the best people I've ever known there.

Carly – Carly's my ride or die. We could've been siblings in a past life or something. She's seen me through some of my hardest times and rolled with me the whole way. If I had to hide a dead body, I would call Carly to help me.

Angela – Angela was in school when we first clicked up and went on to be a successful journalist. She's also an army veteran. We met shortly after she returned from Iraq. Angela's always good company, the world would be a better place if more people were like her.

Phil – Phil loves sports and music and shows and events and things and stuff. He was also in school back then and interning with 'at risk' youth at the city juvenile hall. When he wasn't saving the children, he was rewarding himself for his good deed to society. Phil always knew how to have a good time. We went on to be roommates, I have done some really dumb shit with Phil.

Karly – yes I have two, this is Karly with a K. This girl's a blast. She could drink you under the table then proceed to own the dance floor. A film major, artist, designer, and just overall badass. I adore this girl.

Carson – Carson and I were cut from a similar cloth with a background in graffiti and skateboarding. He was originally from Salinas, California, which I found to be fairly similar to Northern New Mexico. Carson was straightedge for a while and sang in a Hardcore band (that's a genre if you don't know). He eventually strayed from music to pursue tattooing. This guy is insanely talented, there's really not much he can't do.

Dana – Dana is a youthful spirit. She was in school for marketing and usually coming up with funny ideas taken from day to day situations for her homework assignments. Dana was benevolent, always treating people. This girl has bought me a lot of drinks and cab rides. God bless you Dana.

Andrea – Andrea was working at the Hard Rock Cafe while attending school in New Orleans when Hurricane Katrina hit. Needless to say, her life got fucked up and she transferred to SF to be closer to her family in Sacramento. She was annoyed by virtually everything but had a brilliant, sardonic sense of humor about her life situation. She could always make me laugh. We also went on to be roommates alongside Phil and Martin.

For the next two years, I was drunk all the time. If I wasn't working or painting I was drinking (or hung-over), we all were. It was hard not to be, there was always something to get into. This didn't help my already inadequate financial status. Most of the time people picked up my bar tab and I was still broke as fuck. My priorities were screwed up but I still managed to be creative in my day-to-day efforts to achieve what I deemed important. Things like eating out, having art shows, or chasing girls. I crossed paths with a lot of graff writers in the city being out drinking all the time, so I managed to meet folks who had the ins with art openings, warehouse shows etc. It was cool; I went on to have shows with folks or crews I used to read about in magazines back in NM. They were more like art parties, nobody was making killer sales or anything but it was always a good time as well as an opportunity to impress a lady.

If I could invite a girl to come through a show I was having, it was a chance to look cool or slightly more accomplished than I really was. Girls like talent, charisma, confidence, things I was led to believe that I had. Girls also like money (everybody likes money), which I didn't have. So I had to be inventive with my follow up. When the show was over, more often than not, the masses would rally to a nearby bar or club. If I wasn't into it, I'd grab my date for the night, attempt to lose the crowd, get a (cheap) bottle of something and suggest hitting a look out point on the way back to the crib. My favorite spot was the Westin hotel on Union Square. They have those wicked glass elevators attached to the side of the building. You could go up thirty something floors and see the best view of the city on your way up.

Once you reached the top, the mission was to sneak down the hallway unseen to a door that lead out to a maintenance balcony. It was small, big enough to accommodate maybe four people. In the daytime you could see the majority of downtown and most of the surrounding area. After dark it was one of the best high-rise views of city lights you could ask for. My boy, Mark showed me this place. He was a savvy traveling b-boy from back in Albuquerque. Some writers took him up there to fade during one of his stints in SF and he put me on game the first time he came to stay with us on his way to Oregon. He had a twin brother who taught me how to do hand styles back at the Cortez house.

Chicks liked going up to the Westin spot. It was cool, it was different, it was even romantic and it was free. A girl's not going to remember every Tom, Dick and douchebag that takes her to a bar or restaurant, but she might remember that sophisticated thuggish kid who took her trespassing at a high-end hotel. Today, you need a room key to get on the elevators. I didn't just take girls there, I'd go there by myself or with friends.

Reese loved this place, he moved in with us some time after Steve left. He used to go up there and take pictures when he started getting into photography. We hung out up there on his 23rd birthday, just a few hours before saving my neighbor's life.

Our downstairs neighbor, Vince, was a kind of a recluse.

He was cool but didn't talk much. He was a big guy, city kid, wore baggy clothes, kicked his hat to the side, liked to smoke and drink. He was one of us. We all got along. Vince was a night owl; he was usually up late working on his car in the garage underneath our apartment. It wasn't uncommon to come home late and hear him throwing tools around and bumping music at some ungodly hour. So after a night of being out celebrating Reese's birth, we stumble home, through the gate and up the stairs like any other night. But as soon as we walk in the door, the hard stench of gasoline hits us like a brick. We heard Vince's car running when we came in but didn't think anything of it, we were very drunk. Martin and Wade were sleeping and we were concerned about how long the fumes had been coming through the vents from the garage up to our flat.

We opened up windows and went downstairs to tell Vince to call it a night. When we got down there, we found him passed out in the driver's seat with the windows up. There was an empty bottle of tequila on the hood and a hose running from the exhaust to a small gap in the driver side window. There was a moment of hesitation because we were hammered. We felt bad for interrupting Vince's stairway to heaven but we couldn't realistically just let him die in the garage and turn our house into a gas chamber in the process. I figured if it was really his time to go, we wouldn't have shown up when we did. We woke him up, it spooked him. He ran into his apartment and slammed the door. We tried to get him to come out and talk to us but he refused. He said that he was cool and to not worry about it. I turned off the car and chucked the hose.

We didn't see Vince for a couple weeks or so after that, we figured he went somewhere to finish what he started. It was sad to think about but I figured if he genuinely wanted to die, that was his business. We thought about saying something to the landlord or maybe even filing a missing person report but right when we started seriously humoring the idea, Vince showed up. I was walking home from the laundromat one day and there he was, just sitting outside the front of the house puffing on a blunt. He seemed in good spirits, he offered me a pull off the weed and went on talking about whatever, like we had seen each other yesterday. He never said anything about the incident, ever. We all just pretended that it didn't happen.

When we drink, we get drunk. When we get drunk, we fall asleep. When we fall asleep, we commit no sin. When we commit no sin, we go to Heaven. So let's all get drunk and go to Heaven.

—Bruce Aidells

13

It's last call at a crummy dive bar on Polk Street and Karly and I are heading to an after party at a downtown hotel. We after partied a lot back then. It wasn't uncommon to pull all nighters or be stuffing your drunk face with pizza at 3:30 a.m. We hit the store and grabbed a bottle. Like most hotel parties, it didn't take long to get a noise complaint and we continued on our way. We finished our drinks, talked to some homeless folks, smoked a couple cigs and did some good old-fashioned loitering. That shit's fun when you're 22 and wasted. We were stumbling aimlessly when a cab drove past. I flagged it down for Karly, we were going opposite directions so, ladies first. We exchanged good night hugs and I proceeded on my way towards Market Street. I was looking out for another cab but didn't see shit. I had a cell phone at this point but on this night, it just happened to be dead. It was around four a.m and I figured I could wait for an owl bus. If a bus or cab didn't come by, it wouldn't be too long before Muni started running and I could just hop the train.

San Francisco is a city actually quite capable of snoozing. I was posted up at Market and 9th street; there wasn't anyone around except street sweepers and homeless people. No cabs, no busses, I took a seat. Waiting for a bus by yourself, shitfaced in the middle of the night is well, boring. So boring that one might even just fall asleep. Which is exactly what I did, I passed out at the bus stop at the corner of 9th and Market for a little over an hour. Not the absolute worst place to take a power nap but definitely not the best.

When I came to, I was totally discombobulated. I checked my pockets to see if I had been mugged during my inebriated slumber, everything appeared to be in tact. The sun was starting to come up and the train to my neck of the woods was about to be operating. I got up, dusted myself off, and went downstairs to the civic center station to catch the outbound N Judah.

The train pulled up almost as soon as I hit the platform, resurgence! I was back in the game, up until the moment that I passed out for the second time and woke up at Ocean Beach forty blocks past my stop. I then had to wait for the driver to take a break, turn the train around and roll all the way back down Judah to 9th Ave. I literally held my eyes open on the ride back to ensure that I didn't pass out again.

9th Avenue is a relatively steep hill, it wasn't crazy like some San Francisco hills but it was a workout walking up it. There was a bus that went right past the house but I was in no state to do anymore waiting for public transportation. I was crawling by the time I reached the front gate, seriously, like an injured soldier. I had to be at work by eleven o' clock that morning. It was awful at the time, now it makes me laugh.

That same week, I got a call from Jean, inviting me and Reese to Mexico with her and a friend. She was living in Los Angeles at the time attending fashion school and was looking to get out of town for a few days. Her family had a time-share in Puerto Peñasco that was available in the spring. I didn't have the money to go but still gladly accepted the invite. We spent the next couple weeks sorting our work schedules, put aside rent/bills for the next month and caught a bus down south to meet the girls in L.A. We drove in Jean's car from there. I hadn't been to Mexico since I was a kid. This trip was a blast. We had amazing dinners and nights out on the town, went sight seeing, shopping, swimming, four wheeling, caught live music, drank our faces off, popped pharmaceuticals, all that good stuff. All while staying in a high-end resort on the beach. It was like I got to pretend that I was somebody else for week. Although I did in fact have a blast drinking tequila and popping Percocet for days straight, you couldn't pay me to do that shit now. Don't mix liquor and pharmaceuticals; you'll destroy your insides and fucking die.

The next few months were drama, it just seemed to follow me for some reason. Granted, the way I was living could have been attracting it. House parties that went south, bar brawls, too many run ins with the cops and I even managed to get my face cracked open on the 4th of July in North Beach. It was Phil's birthday. I was tagging outside the establishment we were drinking at and an off duty manager came up behind me and slammed my face into the wall. Split my lip open pretty bad, had to get sixteen stitches. Considering I'm British, it's actually quite fitting that an American dude fucked me up on Independence Day, cheers.

My last brush with potential death during this time period was jumping out of an airplane. It was Dana's birthday and she insisted that we all squad up and go skydiving. She did it big, rented a limo with a bar and everything. So we piled into the stretched limousine and drove from San Francisco down to Hollister to literally sign our lives away. True story, they make you sign a contract that states if you're injured or killed, your family and friends cannot take legal action and it's basically your fault for wanting to jump out of an airplane. That being said, I can't deny that shit was cool, terrifying but totally cool. We jumped from 10,000 feet and somersaulted out of the plane so I could see it flying away as I plummeted towards the ground with a complete stranger strapped to my back. It was loud, I figured I'd be shitting my pants up until the parachute came out (if the parachute came out) but to my surprise, my mind was clear. I thought I was on some Wu-Tang shit until I read somewhere a few years later that "Nothing makes you present and mindful like being mere inches away from your own death." Who knew? After about fifteen seconds, the parachute did in fact release and suddenly, it's dead silent. There I was flying through the sky, enjoying a spectacular California view. I made it to the ground in one piece, did a shot of Jagermeister and waited for the rest of the crew to touch down. We drove back to the city, got dropped off at an outer mission bar and got very drunk.

Martin and I had moved to this neck of the woods by this point with Andrea and Phil. Wade took off to L.A and I honestly don't remember where Reese ended up during this time period. He was either living solo in the TL or may have moved in with Justice by now. Justice was a friend from back home who had moved to the East Bay to attend UC Berkeley. She'd come to the city for shenanigans with us pretty often. Justice was truly one of the crew back then. I could give this girl pages worth of an introduction, I love and admire her very much. She's been around since the beginning. She and Reese started dating sometime after they both moved out there.

We used to have parties or folks over often at the 9th Ave house but that was less common at our new digs in the Excelsior. We lived on the top of a wicked hill, which was enough to deter anyone riding public transit. There was no bus that went past this house. Sometimes Martin and I would call somebody to come pick us up at the bottom of the hill because we just didn't have it in us. We didn't have too many options as far as rides; we didn't know that many people with cars. Enter Jamie. Jamie was and still is the best. If she were able, she would stop whatever she was doing to come take care of our degenerate asses. She drove us everywhere (Carly gets major credit here too).

She'd take us shopping, to the laundromat, to pay bills, etc. In addition to being our personal taxi service, she worked at Baskin Robbins at the time and kept our freezer stocked with ice cream daily. We met through mutual friends back at 9th Ave and decided she was a keeper. Fortunately, she felt the same way about us.

The city can be overwhelming at times, it's hard to detach or escape when there's a lot going on around you. When I felt like this, I'd try and make more frequent trips to the East Bay or go down to Santa Cruz and surrounding areas. We used to paint trains down in that neck of the woods, we had affiliates from the area that knew the ropes. Carson had moved back to Salinas for a minute so I'd go and see him occasionally. I met cool folks through Carson but the one that I really connected with was Rob.

Rob was from Visalia, a smallish city just south of Fresno but he would make frequent trips up to Salinas to stay with Carson, they were best friends. It's rare that you can meet someone and genuinely hit it off, like you've been friends for ages. I hadn't clicked with somebody like that since Reese and I met as kids.

Rob was into graffiti like the rest of us, he wrote BOSEK, so we all called him Bo. He was really good, the youngest of a crew of more established cats who took him under their wing. Rob was sort of seeing this girl attending SF State back then, so he'd make a point of hitting me up when he was in the city visiting her. We'd grab dinner, throw a cruise, walk around and tag on shit, it didn't really matter what we were doing, I always liked Bo's company.

After a pretty lousy two-year stint at the Hard Rock Cafe, I finally decided to quit. I had tried a few different positions from host to prep cook to expediter and I was unhappy in every one. After a few months of being on the expo line dealing directly with one of the most difficult kitchens I've ever encountered, I asked to be transferred back to the door to help lead the host team. My request was denied. They told me I could expedite or I could find a new job. So I waited until a wicked lunch rush, the line was full; the cooks were in the weeds. I calmly took off my apron, dropped it on the floor and walked out in the middle of my shift. One of the cooks yelled at me on my way out of the kitchen. "Guerro! What are you doing?! Where are you going?!" I flipped him off and kept on my way out the door. I caught the bus to a bar halfway to my house. I had ten dollars in my pocket and nothing in my bank account. That's enough for a beer I figured. I sat there baby sitting my one drink, trying to make it last as long as I could, pondering what I was going to do. I knew that I had made a less than responsible decision but I had to get out of there. Fuck it, I would find a new job sooner than later.

I actually reached out to my dad during this time. We talked via email a lot, I didn't have a computer or Internet so I would go to the Apple store and use one of the demo models available to the public. My dad was living on government assistance and barely scraping by. I knew he didn't have shit but I figured what the hell. He was an imaginative dude. Maybe he had an idea, an optimistic lie, anything would have been welcome at the time. The old man told me he would do his best to come up with something but suggested to me that I do my best to be creative in the meantime. He'd say, "I know it's hard to be inspired when you feel down and out but try to paint something, pain adds color to your palette." I got *Pain Adds Color* tattooed across my chest on my 23rd birthday. It was Lisa's idea, she even paid for it.

I wasn't actually unemployed for long, luckily it was just a few days before I landed a food running/bar backing gig at a way nicer place called Annabelle's. Annabelle's was at the corner of 4th and Mission, downtown, so I could get off at the Powell St. station and be right there. It was a way easier commute than going all the way to the wharf. I was making better money at Annabelle's and working with a nicer kitchen staff but I was still just working to live. I wanted to be doing more than working and partying but I had difficulty envisioning anything else. I was glad to be making art and partaking in shows around the city but most artists will tell you there's not always money in that hustle. I didn't want to give up but I knew I needed to try something else. Strangely enough, shortly after this manifestation, I received a letter in the mail from my mom, basically expressing that she was concerned about me and my situation.

A phone call is one thing but when you get a letter in the mail, shit is getting real. She proposed the idea of me moving back to New Mexico and attending college in Albuquerque. She said that she would attempt to pay my rent on an affordable apartment and or help out the best she could if I agreed to do so. My mom was broke as fuck. There was no way she could pay my rent but her boyfriend, Harvey, at the time had offered to help out as well. He wasn't doing too hot financially either but they seemed confident that between the two of them, they could pull it off.

My mom really wanted me to go to school. I initially said no but she persuaded me to give it a chance. Worst-case scenario, I could come back to California. I thought it over and decided I would give it a shot. There were things that did sound appealing about the situation. Having my own place and a car sounded pretty dope after years of roommates and public transit. Mom offered me Zoe's kind of run down jeep she had at the time because she was about to go off to school in Boston. I was coming up on twenty-four and did in fact want to be doing something different. I just wanted to do it more on my terms, which was probably never going to happen. The universe was offering me an opportunity. I could swallow my pride and take it or continue down my path of complacency. I went for it, I was confused, nervous and everything else that you feel when change is taking place. Change is hard, even when it's for the best. I stacked a little money, found someone to rent my room at the Excelsior house, rented a van to move what little I was bringing with me and put in my notice at work.

I remember my last cab ride in the city. I was heading home from a roof top party in SOMA. I knew I was leaving in the next few days and I was looking out the window just taking everything in. It's quiet for the first few minutes until the driver breaks the silence.

"So, where ya from?"

"New Mexico, actually heading back there this week."

"Oh yeah? You been out here long?"

"Little over three years, how bout you?"

"Little over twenty, man I'll tell you what, you're gonna miss this place."

"Yeah. Yeah, I know."

"Eh, you'll be back, we'll see you again."

He was right.

I moved to California not to pursue acting but to get out of Albuquerque.

—Minka Kelly

14

Carly and I touched down at my mom and Harvey's place off old Taos Highway early in the morning. Carly rolled with because I didn't even have a driver's license at the time and she had to rent the van for me. So it was probably a good idea that she just went ahead and drove it as well. She managed to get a few days off work and liked the idea of a quick road trip. It was really nice having her there with me for the first few days, we partied it up. I introduced her to old friends, did some touristy shit and showed her around. The time passed quickly and like that, Carl was on a plane back to Cali and it was time to start figuring out what I was doing.

I hopped on it, within a couple weeks, I got my driver's license, registered for classes at a community college in Albuquerque and even found a shitty apartment almost right next door. Turned out my immediate neighbor was a drunk who scrapped with his girlfriend regularly (the cops would show up at my door asking about domestic disturbance often) and my downstairs neighbors were crackheads but hey, I could walk to and from school. Even though my new digs were nothing to brag about, I was determined to style it out and make it as comfortable as

I could. Which I did, I came up on some decent furniture, put up a bunch of art, had a couple guys come through and paint big graffiti pieces on my bedroom wall, the works. Anything I could do to breathe life into the place.

I had lost touch with Albuquerque over the years and more or less forgot how to get around. So I got a part time delivery/catering job to get reacquainted with the surroundings. Besides that, I was just focusing on school. I needed a bunch of general education credits in order to start pursuing anything worth a shit so with the exception of an advanced English class and a couple drawing classes, it basically felt like I was back in high school. I enjoyed being back in a classroom to an extent. Debating, clowning around, arguing with people. I guess old habits die hard. I did some good work though, wrote some good papers, did some bad drawings.

I didn't know too many folks living in the area at this point so I spent a lot of time by myself. Most cats had moved away and stuck it out and the ones that were around were too busy pursuing degrees. My man, Gabe, lived down the street from me so I saw him often even though he was losing his mind in med school. We both smoked a lot of weed back then so we made time to chill and smoke. I had known Gabe since high school. We initially met through Tina. I wasn't socializing with too many other folks besides Chuck's sister, Reese's brother (he moved back from Seattle for a job) and my friend, Rome. Rome was an O.G from one of my early graff crews. He put me on some game alongside people like Hour and the twins. Rome was actually his tag, his real name was Ryan but it was rare that anyone actually called him by his government name. Rome was trying to get clean back then so we mostly just smoked cigs and drank coffee or something non-alcoholic. He secretly went off to rehab out of state a few months after I moved back.

Around the same time, mom fell off as far as being able to float my rent. I knew she wouldn't be able to do it long term and I was impressed as well as grateful that she did what she could. It was crazy not paying rent for those few months. I didn't save any money because I only worked enough to pay for basic day-to-day expenses while attending school. So when mom confessed to me that she just couldn't do it anymore, I had to think up a way to make some extra loot fast. Mom felt bad but she couldn't deny her position and neither could I. Again, I was grateful that she managed to help me while I got settled into school and the new digs.

I picked up a couple extra shifts at work and got a small time weed hustle on the side. One of my downstairs neighbors was a shady cat who worked at a pharmacy. He would steal painkillers from work and sell them to me for cheap or occasionally trade me for weed. I could flip the pills for more than the weed so that was a better hustle. Plus I didn't do pills so I never dipped into my own supply, which wasn't always the case with the weed. I was broke but I was making rent and bills. I didn't need money for much else at the time anyway. I wasn't going out or spending, with the exception of the late night homework stint at the Frontier. The Frontier restaurant is an Albuquerque staple right across from the main UNM campus. It used to be a 24 hour joint but their insurance company threatened to cut them off after years of late night drama.

Everyone has a story about the Frontier. If you've ever been there after a bar, show, party, etc. Chances are you've seen some shit go down. My personal favorite Frontier tale is this one – I'm standing in a line stretching around the block waiting to get into the restaurant. It's a counter service joint so there's usually a line; it's just after 1 a.m. I was coming from a concert at the Sunshine Theatre. I can see inside the place through the big glass windows and doors from where I am. There's an obviously drunk guy acting disorderly and getting into it with a security guard. One thing leads to another and the guy swings on the guard, he misses and stumbles. The security guard's a big dude. He grabs the drunken perpetrator and throws him into the glass door. On contact, the drunk basically projectile vomits into the glass, sending puke ricocheting off the door out into the crowd of people standing in line around him. Mortified and disgusted, the puke sprayed bystanders proceed to jump in and help the security guard beat his ass. It was like a dark comedy skit gone wrong. Today, the Frontier is closed from 1-5 a.m. I remember when they announced they were no longer going to be 24 hours; it was the end of an era.

After losing my late night homework grub hub, the only

thing in the area that served as a substitute for a 2 a.m. snack or really bad cup of decaf, was the sketchy 7-11 at the end of my street. Making the after hours mission to 7-11 always sucked. There were usually bums or junkies lurking, always asking for something or trying to sell me some stolen shit. To this day, this is the only location I've ever been aggressively propositioned by a hooker on the street, after years in the Bay Area! There were actually two of them, young girls probably around my age at the time. I remember they had meth sores all over their faces. They got mad at me and called me a faggot for rejecting their kind offer.

That same week, I was making the trip on foot and some creeper serial killer looking dude pulled over in a bucket and asked if I needed a ride. I flipped out and started yelling crazy shit at him while kicking his car. He peeled off; I picked up a rock and threw it at him as he drove away. I kept one in my hand for the rest of the walk incase he turned around. I hated my neighborhood after that so I started cruising down to Harold's instead. Harold's is a 24 hour laundromat/convenience store on Girard St. It was a couple miles away from my crib but it was worth the cruise to not have to deal with the bullshit. They also sold single cigs back then and the dude behind the counter would occasionally invite me to hotbox his hearse with some really bad weed.

My situation in New Mexico started to feel complacent. I'd been back for a bit over a year and college still felt like high school, I had lost my drive to pursue a degree. I was thinking about dropping out. The only reason I was even still attending class at that point was to slang. I had to repeat an Algebra 2 class and was looking at being held back for a third time because my grade still sucked. I wasn't having it. I offered my teacher a hundred bucks to give me a passing grade and just let me move on. He said no. I offered him more but he still said no. Kids, I'm not suggesting that attempting to bribe your college professor is a good idea, but it's always an option. And I'm confident that somewhere out there, there's a teacher that will take the money.

I left school early that day because I would have rather punched myself in the nuts than go to my drawing class and be forced to sketch a still life of a wood block leaning up against a vase. I walk up to my gate and there's a youngish looking black gentleman standing there in hospital scrubs, smoking a prime time. He introduced himself as one of my new neighbors. His name was Chris, he said he was a medical assistant at UNMH and had just moved from California. We talked for a minute, I let him know it was good to make his acquaintance and continue on my way but not before Chris asks me if I know where to get any weed. I ask him if he's a narc or something to that affect. He laughs and assures me he's not. I break him off a dime and tell him he can pay me later since we're neighbors. He points out his apartment, I point out mine. The entire complex consisted of fifteen in total. We shake hands and go our separate ways.

The next day I'm at home catching up with some folks I hadn't seen in a while - Rich, Mac, Sam and Kevin. There we are cracking beers and rolling blunts when there's an unexpected knock at the door. I ask who it is, turns out it's my new neighbor, Chris. I open the door to find homeboy standing there in some type of uniform! He looked like something between a cop and a security guard. All I knew is yesterday he was wearing scrubs claiming to be a medical assistant getting weed from me and today he shows up unannounced in a uniform to supposedly pay for the weed I had fronted him the day before. This dude was some kind of official, or some kind of stupid.

Let me shed some light on the guys I'm with. Rich is a sophisticated thug type. He's sharp, clean cut, has money, likes drugs and usually has a gun on him. Kevin is currently awaiting trial for a list of charges ranging from dealing to gun possession and who knows what else. He's irritable and paranoid. Mac is an overall laid back cat, but he's a stalky laid back cat that spends a lot of time at the gym. Mac has man tits, he could hurt you. Sam is also a laid back stoner type but in a scheming and plotting kind of way. Sam is a man of focus and commitment. And then there's me. So Chris shows up unexpectedly and gets an uncomfortable drop on our little gangster party. I pull him inside, lock the door and demand an explanation for the outfit. He chuckles and claims that he also works security at the hospital. I'm not buying it, I'm too caught off guard and never heard of anything like that. I'm also embarrassed that he's pulling this out of left field shit in front of my company. He offers up the money he owes me, I tell him fuck that, he can keep it. He apologizes and swears he's a security guard on his way to work, which is why he stopped by dressed in uniform. It just isn't sitting right though. If nothing else, I was irritated that he would do something so stupid. Why wouldn't he mention that he also works security during our first encounter the day before? I turn to the guys who are also sketched out. "I'm kinda trippin guys, what should we do?"

Rich picks a freshly packed bowl up off the coffee table, takes some cocaine out of his pocket and sprinkles a little on top. He hands it to Chris and says, "Smoke that." Chris chuckles again while trying to plead his redundant case. Rich tells him to shut the fuck up and clarifies that he doesn't have a choice. Kevin stands in front of the door and informs him that if he wants to leave, he has to smoke the whole thing. Mac, Sam and I all agree. Chris lets out a sigh of defeat, "Man ya'll are crazy", he says before ripping the pipe several times until it's cashed. It was a bootleg Albuquerque version of *Training Day*. Kevin steps aside and we send him on his way. He was already stumbling out the door holding on to the rail with both hands going down the stairs. After the paranoia wore off, we were laughing about it. The next time I saw Chris he was still spinning the same story and claimed that work that day was awful and extremely difficult.

I actually apologized but told him that he had made a bad decision. Everyone around here was sketched out because everyone was doing some sketchy shit, act accordingly God damnit.

I got a call from Bo a few days later, I told him about the incident with Chris. He thought it was hysterical. Bo was one of the people from back in California I had kept in consistent touch with since returning to New Mexico, he called or texted often. Most times it was just jokes and talking shit but we'd have the occasional serious catch up about music, girls, graffiti and everything in between. We had been talking for almost an hour when his service started breaking up. He was driving home from the Bay and was going through a bad reception area. I told him to just hit me back later in the week and we'd pick up where we left off. I hung up, still laughing to myself about the inside jokes we were throwing around.

A few days later I got a call from Carson. I was at a restaurant getting lunch with some folks in Santa Fe but I stepped out to take the call. I hadn't talked to him in a while and I wanted to at least say hi and maybe set up a later date to catch up. I figured maybe Bo had told him about our most recent convo and he felt inspired to hit me up as a result. "Whatup man!" I howled into the phone. "Hey bro." His response sounded melancholy, like he was tired or drained. I picked up on his somber tone immediately so I inquired.
    "What's good player? You cool? What's goin on?"
    "Uh yeah man I'm alright."
    I could tell at this point that he'd been crying.
    "It's just that, Kit, Bo killed himself yesterday."

I froze, stopped dead in my tracks like a statue. When shock hits you that hard, it's literally difficult to move. After a moment of silence I brought myself to say that was impossible, that I had just talked to him a few days earlier and there was no fucking way. We were laughing our asses off, he was fine. There was no fucking way! Carson agreed that he seemed in good spirits the last time they spoke as well. He said he was sorry to be the bearer of bad news and assured me that there wasn't any mistake, Bo was gone.

This was before social media took over the world. Myspace was a thing and Facebook was in its beginning stages but we weren't paying attention to any of that shit. Carson knew I wouldn't find out unless he called me. I freaked out but I managed to thank him for calling, told him I loved him and said we would talk in the next couple days. I was standing in the middle of a parking lot. I took a seat on a curb and just started to come undone as the news began to set in. I got up after a few minutes, went back inside the restaurant, paid for my food, said peace to the folks I was with and went to sit in my car.

I just sat there and cried for a while. I couldn't drive, I couldn't do shit except just sit there and sob. I had lost quite a few folks and acquaintances by this point but it had been a while since something hit that close to home. It's not uncommon to humor a guilt driven thought process under these circumstances. You might think, shit, what if I had said something they needed to hear or made them feel something they needed to feel at the time. That's bullshit though, the fact is Bo more than likely decided he was done weeks before he even called me. Looking back, I think he was just calling to say peace. I'm grateful that he included me in the last days of his journey.

Robert Ian Sawyer hung himself in August of 2007. He was twenty-one years old. Rest in peace homie, you're missed by many and thought of often.

I am one of those who never knows the direction of my journey until I have almost arrived.

—Anna Louise Strong

15

Shortly after Bo passed, I got hit with some more bad news, I went to get a checkup at a local clinic and it turned out I had a hernia. I'm not sure how it happened, possibly during the move back to NM. I was going to need surgery and the doctor advised that I get it dealt with ASAP. I didn't have health insurance and had no idea how I was going to pull off a surgical operation with a pre-existing condition. I already had medical debt from back in California. Luckily, my friend, Phay, was able to hook me up with a guy who helped me get on some form of Medicaid. It was a small program, which was dismantled shortly after I was able to qualify but they kept the patients they already had. It was basically a miracle. I'm forever grateful to Phay for that. I officially had to leave school and quit my job.

I gave away my furniture and packed up the few things I was keeping in the mini van I was driving at the time. I had a little Corolla after Zoe's jeep crapped out but things kept going wrong with it and I couldn't afford the upkeep. My mom's friend was selling a spacious mechanically sound mini van for $1,200.00. The only catch was that the air conditioning didn't work and the windows didn't roll down.

I wasn't planning on having the car for long so I didn't want to put any money into it. Cruising around Albuquerque in the summertime with no AC and the windows up was like riding in an oven. The van served its purpose though. It moved my life back to Santa Fe and I even managed to sell it for what I bought it for, which is what I needed to live on while recuperating from surgery at my mom's new spot over by *Santa Fe High*. It's too bad that money had to go towards keeping me afloat, otherwise it could have potentially gone towards a ticket back to England for Max and Helen's wedding. Which unexpectedly turned out to be the same week as my dad's funeral. Lisa and Zoe made it out there along with some other family for the wedding but the old man suddenly passed from a heart attack and everyone had to come together to organize two ceremonies. Lisa called me, she tried to keep it together at first but she started breaking down as the words actually left her mouth. Dad was gone.

Losing a parent is different than losing a friend. Perhaps that element of irreplaceability is intensified. My relationship with my dad had been mostly via email over the last few years so it wasn't the usual immediate feeling of 'oh shit, I'm never going to see that person again'. I consulted my dad about almost everything. He was kind of like a diary that wrote back. I would usually ask for advice in relation to whatever I was babbling about and even if I didn't love the answer, the old man had a way of making everything sound like it was going to be alright. My Dad was one of the most brilliant and screwed up people I ever knew.

From his fantastic talents and achievements to his darkest struggles and failures. He was beautifully human, just perfectly imperfect.

I'm very much my father's son. I see a lot of similarities between the two of us, which frightens me as well as makes me happy. No matter what I did or how low I sank, he always assured me that I was on the right track and he was proud of me. He apologized a million times for the way things panned out, he always had a hard time forgiving himself. Even though I forgave him time and time over. It's sad to think that dad passed on alone with virtually nothing but I'm confident that he was relatively at peace. He had finally quit smoking and drinking, made amends anywhere he could as well as became fairly spiritual in his later days. I miss his letters. I still ask him for a hand or a shove in the right direction once and a while. I don't know if he hears me but it can't hurt to ask.

The healing process from the hernia surgery was going to be about a month and proved to be a little tough. I was bedridden and couldn't be up and about for long. I was high on prescribed painkillers half the time, watched a lot of TV, ate a lot of soup and soft foods because I had to be weary of my digestive system. I lost 10-15 pounds. When I finally bounced back I started working on a new body of paintings and got another part time service industry job. I didn't have a car at this point but my mom was nice enough to let me use hers fairly often.

When I couldn't use hers, my friend, Monique would usually catch my back. Monique worked 9-5 at a bank and would let me use her car while she was at work as long as I picked her up by the time she got off. She really held me down back then. My girl, Kim, gets recognition here too. Kim and I went back to the Cortez house days, she was living in Sacramento when I was in San Francisco and we'd catch up occasionally out there. The visits were mellow since she was pregnant back then. She was still based in Sacramento but sadly was visiting NM for an indefinite amount of time due to her brother passing away. So we spent a lot of time together during this period. Between my mom and the girls, I always had a ride to or from work, or anywhere really. Thanks girls, I love y'all.

I didn't want to get stuck back in the service industry for long so I started looking for a different gig, preferably in the art field. My friend, Liz was working for a reputable gallery on Canyon Road in Santa Fe at the time. I told her I was looking for a change of scenery and she was nice enough to pull some strings and score me a paid art handling internship.

I was excited at first but it didn't take long to figure out that working behind the scenes of a prestigious art venue was just fancy manual labor. Lifting, Hauling, packing, wrapping, drilling, spackling, etc. In addition to the pressure of handling heavy and expensive art pieces. It just wasn't as cool as I hoped it would be.

The director of the gallery at the time was a young, sharp, attractive lady, always dressed to the nines and ready to make that big sale. She used to say, "The only thing glamorous about this job, is your outfit." I finished the internship and decided I didn't want to work in an art gallery but I did want to hang and curate art shows. I looked into a space downtown that was willing to rent me a portion of their establishment for a month. I scored a grant to pay the rent and I started recruiting artists from Santa Fe and Albuquerque to be part of my first curatorial project. After a month or so of studio visits, I put together a lineup of twenty artists. The show went well, the turn out was great.

I decided to do it bigger and better within the year. I found an amazing space that I didn't even have to rent, it was run by an artist collective that donated it to folks who got on a wait list. Lofton and I spent a couple months organizing the show; I bust my ass on this one. I was a little disorganized on opening night as well as running late. Which led to me getting pulled over, which led to me getting arrested for a warrant I didn't know I had.

It was for a failure to appear in court for a damn traffic citation that I did in fact attempt to deal with not once, but twice. The cop that cited me decided to process the paper work long after the incident and the woman at the office assured me that if it hadn't been done by that point in time, it was probably thrown out or lost. I called to inquire one last time after that and they told me they still had nothing on file. I was in Monique's car when I got pulled over and due to the fact that I was well mannered and cooperative, the cops were actually nice enough to let me call her and explain she needed to try and come pick it up ASAP or they would impound it. She got there in a timely fashion and said she would bail me out. I had never been to jail in Santa Fe but I imagined it couldn't be too different from Albuquerque.

I was so bummed on the ride there. I couldn't believe I was going to miss my opening. I asked the cop if he could put in a word to the officials at booking and ask them to allow me to stay in holding until Monique bailed me out. Being moved to population would add more time and hassle to the process. He sympathized to an extent and said he would try. I got processed and thrown in a holding cell with a couple of drug dealers from Española who had just been busted with a kilo of cocaine. They eventually got moved.

For the next couple hours I just sat there and stared at the concrete walls, still in awe that I was missing my show. One of the C.O's informed me that if I didn't get bailed out soon they would have to move me to gen pop. Monique came through, I'm eternally grateful to her for that. Bailing people out of jail is a colossal pain in the ass. I was locked up for about 5-6 hours, long enough to miss the art opening but still able to get to the bar for post shenanigans. I linked up with Lofton and a group of folks who were featured in the show. They were disappointed for me but said that it was a fantastic event and congratulated me on a job well done. I got hammered; I figured I earned it.

Regardless of my trials and tribulations since returning to New Mexico I still ended up back at square one. I was twenty-five and living at my mom's house with no car and a shitty part time job. So I took the little money I had and decided to go back to California. New Mexico had run its course for the time being and I missed the city. Martin had moved into a place downtown with a couple of friends from Albuquerque and I'd be able to hit their couch for an indefinite amount of time. Lisa moved out there with her best friend, Amanda (she's like my other sister) a year or so before I left. They had a full house with a couple other girls but they accommodated me when need be. Tina, Kai, and my man, JT, all took me in as well. I occasionally scored a sublet. It was pretty breezy; I always had a comfortable place to stay.

Lisa and Amanda got me a weed-trimming gig and JT hooked me up with an on-call job working the door at a bar in the Western Addition. I wasn't making enough to commit to moving back but I was definitely making enough to float. Being in the city with no rent or significant bills was dope. I wanted to ride it out for a while. A couple months in, death reared its head once more. This time it was Reese's dad. He had been living in San Diego and battling cancer for the last couple years all while still trying to run a business and bounce back from a financial mishap.

Reese had relocated to SD to help with all the above. He and his dad were really close. I'd known his old man since we were tykes, I rolled down to San Diego to help him pack up shop and move back to the Bay. We spread his dad's ashes in the ocean before we left. It was a heavy trip but we tried to make the most of it. Shortly after returning to the city, we lost Martin's mom to the same shit, fuck cancer.

Martin's dad had passed a year or so before, I don't remember from what. Most people would probably fall apart if they lost both their parents within the span of a couple years but Martin's a rock. He stayed on point at work and the whole nine. Seriously, one of the strongest dudes I know. He had to roll out to New Mexico to clear out his mom's house and asked me to roll with. So I hit the road again. He had siblings in Orange County and Phoenix so we made stops along the way to visit with the family. Again, heavy trip but we managed to have a good time under the circumstances.

I nestled back into San Francisco for a couple months but work eventually slowed down and I started thinking it might be time for another change of scenery. Carly had moved out to Honolulu not long after I made the move back to NM and although Phil and I had actually been to visit once before we had always talked about me coming back for a proper stay. This seemed like as good a time as any. So I copped a one-way ticket to Hawaii. I had to catch Caltrain from the city to San Jose where my flight was departing at some ungodly hour of the morning so I had to sleep in the San Jose airport. That shit was pretty wack.

Carly scooped me up at the Honolulu airport. I had done all the tourist shit the first time around with Phil, sight seeing, snorkeling, Waikiki, Pearl Harbor, etc. So I was more intent on just chilling out this trip, spending time on the beach and all that good stuff. I had decided I wanted to put together a book project, something along the lines of an autobiographical portfolio. I don't know, something to validate my existence up to this point. Call it a quarter life crisis. I put something together over the course of the next couple weeks. Carl helped me out, I called it *Pain Adds Color*. It was self published and sold on the Internet for more than it was worth. If you purchased one, I apologize and am grateful.

I did eventually get a royalty check for that bad boy for sixty bucks. Chuck's sister just happened to be in Honolulu at the same time I was, she was visiting an aunt who lived on the army base. I was closer with her than I was with Chuck at this point. We had fun together out there; it was good to see a homie from back home. A month passed and I thought about sticking around longer, maybe getting a job and settling into Carl's living room but the reality is that I was living out of a suitcase and had no future plan in sight besides being a drunken beach bum. So I took the funds I had left, and got another one-way ticket from Hawaii back to New Mexico. I had been away for about six months and started feeling like it was time to stabilize once more.

There is nothing so stable as change.

—Bob Dylan

16

When I touched down back in NM I had nothing, so I hopped into another restaurant gig and started from scratch. I saved a little money and bought a hooptie for a grand. I stayed with my mom for the last month or so that she had her place by the high school before she actually took off to Arizona for a potential business opportunity. Lisa had just relocated back to Santa Fe and was living with Amanda's sister. They had a spare room so they let me stay with them for a little while.

Lisa and I started looking for a new place together. Turned out an old friend of hers had a nice place for rent in midtown and was willing to give us a homie price on it. It took us a minute to furnish and style out but it was pimp by the time we were done. Some other folks made the move back from California around the same time, amongst them were Reese, Justice, Rome, and my old roommate from the East Bay, Dave.

Dave made jewelry and was working on opening a gallery on Canyon Road. The space he was looking to rent had a showroom and a cafe attached to the back. He invited me to come and curate shows at the gallery and said I could work the cafe in the mean time. It all fell into place pretty fast. I met and worked with some great artists through that place. It was a good time but it was short lived. Less than a year in, he and his business partner were having financial complications and were looking to downsize wherever possible, they couldn't afford to pay me anymore. Shit happens.

Around this same time, Jean's Family started a disaster restoration business and invited me to come work for them. It wasn't great but it was a job. Making the transition from the art field back to manual labor was a bitch and I eventually inquired about a marketing position instead. Jean's sister, Abby, was nice enough to grant my request. Marketing was better in the sense that I didn't have to do much besides dress nice and drive around town in a company vehicle but the money wasn't as good. I figured I'd stick it out for a while until something else came along.

Outside of work, I was shifting my creative focus towards music. I clicked up with this cat, Damian, through his wife, who was a good friend at the time. Damian and I shared a passion for rap with an emphasis on the Bay Area. He had a makeshift studio at his crib with some decent equipment and the first time we attempted to compose some shit together, it came out tight. We were just messing around, nobody really had any expectations but it sounded good so we ran with it. We put together an instrumental project and eventually started reaching out to rappers. Thanks to the Internet, it's not difficult to contact people. We started talking with golden era Bay Area rap artists about collaborating with us. Emails turned into phone calls, phone calls turned into meetings. We had a record release party, shot a music video, the whole package, it was a blast.

We tried to push what we were doing on local folks but nobody really gave a fuck. I didn't really care; I was producing for some of my favorite artists. Damian and I went on to produce several albums together but eventually parted ways due to creative differences.

Apart from music and work, I had finally attempted to take a stab at a relationship for the first time in my adult life. I said I wasn't going to touch on sexual encounters but that being said, that's really all I had since I was a teenager. There hasn't been talk of another relationship since Tina because there wasn't another one. I'm 27-28 at this point and I've become accustomed to either being alone or just moving from one girl to another. They say variety is the spice of life.

I was really just insecure with an inferiority complex. I wasn't an asshole, or at least I didn't mean to be. I genuinely enjoyed the company of almost all the women I spent time with. I didn't want to disrespect anybody, but I didn't want to settle down either, I didn't even know how. I thought I was just being cool by hanging out, having fun, going to movies, shit like that. I didn't realize I was acting boyfriend-ish.

The problem with acting boyfriend-ish when you're not someone's boyfriend is, more often than not, girls catch feelings. Guys do this too; it's a side effect of being human. I was trying to stay committed to being on some player shit but accidentally ended up in a relationship with Renee. I think we only hooked up a couple times before she informed me that she didn't do that kind of shit unless things were basically exclusive. I should have dipped right then and there but I'm shallow and wanted things to be on my terms. I wanted to hook up with Renee again so I agreed to shack up for the sake of possibly nothing more than a sexual dilemma. We managed to squeeze something meaningful out of it here and there over time. We were on and off over the next year or so. We didn't have too much in common and had difficulty communicating. I think we got along with each other's families better than we did with each other. I tried to embrace being in a relationship but something was missing. I liked the idea of me and Renee more than the reality. I was actually pretty upset when we split but I think it stemmed from the fact that I felt like I was incapable of being in a relationship. All that being said, Renee is lovely, really, there's a lucky man out there that will make it work with her. She's practically angelic with a heart of gold; beautiful, very sweet girl.

Lisa's latest relationship during this time was going well and although it hadn't been long, she had plans to move in with my now brother in law, James. Justice took her place and we eventually moved to a different spot over on Hickox Street. It was just down the way from the old Cortez house. Justice was a good roommate; she was present and helpful through my breakup with Renee. She was still going through similar issues with Reese. They broke up and had been back and forth since returning to NM. Reese and I had started working on putting out a clothing line together and living with Justice was something of a conundrum. It was difficult for him to separate business and personal baggage. I sympathized but it began to take a toll on our work relationship. Between that and other issues like creative disputes and financial complications, I got tired and eventually threw in the towel. Going into business with friends is challenging. Our clothing endeavor was really well received though; it lasted about a year. We called it *Pain Adds Color*

Death was still hanging around but hadn't hit too close to home in some time, until we lost Rome. I don't recall if he relapsed and was drunk or if he was just on one, but shortly after returning to NM, he had a fateful night out in Albuquerque. It started with initially scaling a building to hit a tag and gradually led to attempting to sneak into the backside of a downtown club via their balcony. He slipped, fell three stories and landed on his head. I flew down to UNM Hospital with my man, Loren, as soon as we caught wind of what happened. It was the middle of the night and we were told he wasn't going to make it. He was on life support because his family had to officially pull the plug, but he was gone by the time we got there. They let us go in the room to say goodbye. That shit was crazy, he looked like fucking Frankenstein, you could see where they had tried to patch him up but he was a mess. His eyes were pale and almost transparent. If the eyes are the windows to the soul, Rome's soul had left his body. I couldn't be in the room for long. I cried and hugged him for a moment but I didn't want to see him like that.

Ryan 'Romer' Walters passed away in May of 2011 on the eve of his 31st birthday. Rest in peace player, you're missed by many and thought of often.

Cab drivers are living proof that practice does not make perfect.

—Martin Fischer

17

I had almost given up on looking for a different job when a friend informed me that the local cab company was hiring. I actually knew a guy who drove for them and learned that he would be training me if I decided to apply. Sounded simple enough. I had quit smoking weed (and cigarettes) for a while, which was helpful because I had to take a physical and pass a drug test. When it was all said and done I was officially on the road in a run down Crown Vic taxi from seven a.m. to three p.m. Five days a week. They didn't need night drivers at the time and I didn't really mind having to work days. I had been doing the 9-5 grind for the last few months so it was an easy transition.

I didn't particularly want to work graveyard hours anyway. The catch is that's where the money was. Most times I was just taking tourists to and from the airport. Occasionally I would have to go to Albuquerque, some days I just sat in a parking lot with a book or a painting I was working on. Other times I was dealing with way more than I ever signed up for. Like, taking severe alcoholics to the store at eight in the morning and having to purchase a bottle for them because they're still drunk from the night before and the cashier won't sell to them. I was conflicted at first but these motherfuckers would be shaking, begging and offering me extra money. I figured what the hell, they need their fix, I need the money, and I need them out of my cab so I can get on to the next fare.

It might be a junkie attempting to check into a local help center that claims to be full so they ask you to drop them off at a seedy motel and they'll just detox there. Or maybe a hospital call, picking up a battered, crying woman and playing therapist the whole ride back to their trailer park barrio where you have another call to pick up a dope dealer. The dope dealer's not going far, just down the way to the next project building and wants you to wait with the car running while he handles business. Then it's off to the jailhouse where some poor bastard can't get a ride home after being released. And sometimes, the occasional walk of shame where you pull up and catch a homie leaving a certain someone's house after a night out. Folks would hop in the car, see me and be like, "oh shit, yo man I'll throw you a fat tip if you forget that you ever picked me up here." Sure buddy, your secret's safe with me.

Then every once and a while, you'd have your slightly more intimate encounters, like Robert. Robert was one of my regulars, an old retired alcoholic. I'd pick him up, take him to the liquor store, get a bottle of scotch and he'd throw me a twenty if I let him open it in the back seat on the way home. I laid down some ground rules and assured him if we ever got popped I was going to play stupid. Sometimes he would just chill in the car for a while after I pulled up to his crib to drop him off. He'd tell me to keep the meter running. One day I asked him why he was so adamant about drinking in the car as opposed to waiting until he got home. Or why he chose to stay in the car with the meter running, outside his front door. He said he liked having someone to drink with, even though I wasn't actually drinking. He just wanted someone to talk to while sipping on his bottle. He confessed that he had asked other drivers to let him drink in the car and they had all said no. Obviously for good reason, it was sketchy allowing him to do it but I needed the money and I figured the chances of getting caught were slim enough. I actually made a point of being a little more attentive on those rides with Robert after he told me that. I figured if he was literally paying me to be something along the lines of a drinking buddy, it was courteous to at least try and give homie his money's worth.

Then there was Bridgette. I found Bridgette at a cheap motel in midtown. She was a middle-aged woman in transition, going through a divorce and in a custody battle over her son. She had a ton of luggage; I could barely fit it all in the car. When I inquired about her destination, she started crying and asked if we could just drive. I thought that shit only happened in movies. Being mindful of the fact that she was upset, I politely explained to her that she had to pick a drop off spot sooner than later or we'd be looking at an expensive cruise. The cab company charged for time and distance and was overpriced to begin with. I almost never charged anyone for time, just ran the meter for distance. Regardless of my efforts to take care of folks, it didn't take long to ring up what felt like an inordinate ride. The cars were all connected to the system at headquarters so the dispatcher knew if the meter was on or off. Bridgette confessed that although it wasn't her first choice, she was headed to the women's shelter. She had nowhere else to go and was blowing the last of her money on the cab ride. She was told they would take her in for free and help her get on her feet. When we arrived, they told us they could just about accommodate her but not her belongings. They said there simply wasn't room for it. She cried and pleaded with them but they just got irritated and told her that it wasn't possible or up for discussion. I tried to help but they shut me down as well. My trunk and back seat were packed full of her shit, I called my boss and explained the situation. He told me to leave it on the street and get on with my next fare. I asked the women at the shelter for any alternative or helpful suggestions but they basically said the same thing my boss did. I was pretty shocked that nobody wanted to help.

So I took her stuff to my house. I know it sounds funny but I couldn't think of anything else. This chick's life was falling apart, I wasn't going to leave what she had on the street. I kept her things in my living room for about a month and returned them to her when she actually had a place to put them. She kept me posted about her progress around finding work and getting back on her feet. She eventually moved away to Colorado, I think she worked things out with her husband and got her family back together. She used to call me every now and then just to say hi and tell me I was an angel.

Then there was Rita. I picked her up at a decent motel where she had been staying for about a week. She was a traveling nurse and needed a few things from the store. I rolled to a nearby supermarket, let her out and said I would circle the parking lot. When she got back in the car the only thing she had was a tall bottle of vodka. "Liquid lunch today?" I asked, half joking. "Not entirely", she replied. She reached into her purse and took out a prescription container full of Oxycontin. "Yikes, getting the party started early", I continued with a striving to be humorous tone. "Nah, this party's long overdue." I could hear sadness and a hint of anger in her voice. I blanked for a moment because I was caught off guard but after quickly wrapping my mind around the now awkward situation, I started asking questions. Pretty unimaginative shit like, what happened? Could I maybe help at all? She chuckled, told me I was sweet but assured me that nobody could help her at this point.

When we got back to her motel she asked me if I would walk her to her room. I graciously inquired as to why because my mind started going weird places. Is this bitch a serial killer who lures unsuspecting taxi drivers to her motel room with a suicidal sob story?

"Look, for whatever reason, you're the last person I'm going to see or talk to before checking out of this shit hole. I'm sorry to put this on you, I just don't want to go up there alone."

I sighed, fuck it, fingers crossed. We walked past the front desk but there wasn't anyone there. When we got to her room, she opened the door all the way so I could see inside. It looked like a bomb hit it, housekeeping hadn't been up in there for days. She placed her bottle and pills on the bedside table then turned to me and gave me a hug. It was one of those tight hugs that damn near cuts off your oxygen, the kind of hug you might give someone if you thought it was actually fitting to be your last. She told me thank you, apologized again and wished me a better day. I asked if she'd let me take her to a help center or check her into somewhere. I didn't want to interfere but I was involved at this point whether I liked it or not. She told me that this is what she wanted. I wrote my phone number down and told her if she had a change of heart or needed anything that she could call me.

I walked past the front desk again on my way out, this time someone was there. I decided to tell the receptionist the deal. I felt kind of bad but Rita wasn't the only one I felt for. What about the person who has to find her? I told the motel employees they should just call the cops and tell them to please be gentle with her. I figured from that point, it would go down however it was supposed to. I left and went on with my day, it was weird. I thought about Rita over the next couple weeks. I checked the newspaper, looked at the police notes, obituaries, scouted the net a little, anything that might provide information to unanswered questions but I didn't find anything.

Months passed and although it still crossed my mind, I had stopped digging for information. Then one day, completely out of the blue, I got a call from a number I didn't recognize. It turned out to be Rita. She was calling from a rehabilitation center in Arizona. She told me a crazy story about the cops showing up after she went through with it and had to be rushed to the emergency room to have her stomach pumped. She said it had been a rough couple months but at the end of the day she was actually relieved to be alive and sober. She said she held on to my number and was waiting for the right time to call me. She told me I saved her life and wanted to thank me one more time. Turned out she had a little boy and was grateful that he wasn't going to grow up without a mom. Heavy stuff. I told her I'd do it again and was really glad to hear that she was alive and well.

I could tell more weird cab stories but let's move on to the next series of unfortunate events, starting with Lofton passing away. I mentioned earlier that he had an addiction to pharmaceuticals as well as smoked a pack of cigarettes almost every day. But he also had a really unhealthy diet. He never exercised or did anything to moderate the damage. I used to worry about his well-being but you couldn't tell Lofton anything about his lifestyle. One thing led to another and his immune system eventually just gave out. He was in bed next to his girlfriend at the time and supposedly rolled over on to the floor. She couldn't get him to come to, so she called an ambulance. I was told he was coherent for a second during the ride to the hospital but he was gone by the time I got there with Reese, Abby and Justice.

It was almost exactly one year to the day since Rome passed. I don't actually want to touch on the details of standing over Lofton's death bed. I'd rather talk about the fact that he was an important person in my life. How he was a truly irreplaceable teacher and friend. The countless nights I spent in his studio, stretching and sanding canvas, making and mixing paint, sketching, painting, learning, talking, laughing, smoking, arguing, watching the sunrise, we were both insomniacs. Sometimes when I hit a creative block with a project, I tell him to quit being a dick and help me out. Then I remember he would have told me to quit three steps before I got to that point anyway, so I'm screwed.

James Blackstone Lofton passed away in May of 2012. He was thirty six. Rest in peace Sensei, you're missed by many and thought of often.

I couldn't pay proper respects to everyone who came and went along the way. There's too many but for what it's worth, I want to acknowledge and remember Serena, Scott, Lanice, Bez, Alec, Otis, Mariah, Joe, Siren, Ellie, Stefani, Will, Kyle, Bram, Jess and Zack. Rest in peace y'all, much love.

I was planning on my future as a homeless person. I had a really good spot picked out.

—Larry David

18

year or so passed and our lease was coming to an end. Justice had taken a new job in Albuquerque and was fitting to relocate. I tried to replace her but to no avail. I didn't have anywhere else lined up but had a friend who was almost done building a guesthouse on his property at the time. He said it would be done and available by the time I needed to move. He also said he'd work with me on the deposits if need be. Naturally, the place wasn't done in time and I didn't successfully line up anywhere else or stack the money to do so. I got a storage unit and floated around for a minute. I had quit driving a taxi and started working with the New Mexico film industry painting sets when I could. The work wasn't consistent but since I didn't have rent and bills attached to a house, I could swing it. I was still selling art and getting by.

Shortly after the last film job ended, I got an invitation to go to Austin, Texas. An old friend out there had a room open up in her house that needed a new occupant. She knew my situation so she asked if I'd be interested in a change of scenery before offering it up to a local crowd. I accepted the invite but it was short lived. I couldn't find a job and was back in Santa Fe a couple months later, just shy of my 30th birthday.

By the time most folks turn thirty, they have a degree, a spouse, a kid (or one on the way) a dog, a new car and a mortgage. I had an '01 Maxima and a storage unit. Let's take a moment to reflect on our crappy life decisions… Now let's take a moment to freak out about the fact that life never works out the way you think it will…Welcome back. Feeling better? Me neither. Fantastic. Moving on. I was starting from scratch, again. I began looking for a job, again. I couldn't find anything, again. Actually I probably could have gotten a shitty low paying serving job or something but I was over service industry at the time. I was already homeless and didn't have shit. Why be homeless without shit and a part time job that doesn't pay anything. I could hustle that kind of money. I decided I'd do just that until something desirable came along.

The next year was ridiculous. I did hustle up but I never stacked enough to get a new place and somewhere along the way I just got used to being homeless. I managed to pay my storage unit every month amongst other day-to-day expenses. I was still thinking about possibly leaving NM again. When it came down to it, I had no idea what I was doing and my life had been so chaotic and unstable that the thought of actually getting my shit back together was almost intimidating. Looking back, I had more or less given up on myself. I still painted my ass off though, as it was my only real source of income. I made a shit ton of art back then. Word about my situation spread over time and people started hitting me up to house sit or watch their pets. So more often than not, I actually had a place to stay.

Sometimes it was a hovel, sometimes it was a mansion, other times it was a shady motel room or my mom's office chair. Sometimes it was a couch and every once and a while, I would just have to sleep in my car. But either way, it was a place to paint and sleep.

Towards the end of that summer, I was offered a temporary gig supervising a community service program through the Santa Fe Teen Court. I'm no role model but the kids were in a position to learn something. It was a cool project. I think I inspired some kids to not be criminals, or at least be better criminals. Towards the end of the year, I was burnt on hopping around, I needed a place to stabilize and figure out a more calculated move. Chuck had a place in Albuquerque with a guest room at the time, so against my better judgment, I asked if I could occupy it temporarily if I threw him some money. He said I could move in for a couple months, that's all I needed. That's around the time I met Chanel, and that's when everything changed.

Your task is not to seek love, but merely to seek and find all the barriers within yourself that you have built against it.

—Rumi

19

I originally met Chanel at a house party but we didn't interact much. We ended up working together at a restaurant shortly after and the dominos started falling from there. She was gorgeous, charismatic and straight up hilarious. She could make me laugh to the point of tears. I remember our first date. We spent the entire day together; it was some Hollywood shit. She helped me unload my storage unit and move what I was keeping into Chuck's place. I couldn't believe that. Everybody's your friend until you need to move some shit. Chanel voluntarily helped me move, organize, or throw away everything I owned. She barely knew me. This girl was special. We moved in together a couple months later. It was fast but I needed out of Chuck's house and we were great together. I was nervous but it seemed doable. We found a fresh little spot downtown Santa Fe. It needed some work but we gave it that and then some. We transformed that place, it was pimp. And we lived happily ever after, the end.

No not really, because this is real life and there are no fucking happy endings in real life. The catch to this otherwise perfect love story is that Chanel, like most people, had a little crazy in her. Her crazy knew just how to shake my crazy, which made her crazier, which made me crazier, until we were both in a crazy craze of craziness. That, in a nutshell, is most relationships. When we were good, we were incredible. When we were bad, we were just awful. I blame myself for the most part. When it came down to it, I didn't know how to be a solid partner. I didn't understand the importance of making someone feel secure in a relationship. I wanted her to be okay with everything I did or had done. It bothered me that certain things bothered her. I was selfish and couldn't make the necessary sacrifice. I had started smoking weed and cigarettes again as well, which she didn't do.

She loved me almost unconditionally and tolerated me at my worst. She inspired me creatively and was always supportive. She was a tremendous gift that I simply wasn't ready to receive. She wanted me to be better, happier, healthier, etc. Things that were outside of my comfort zone.

Even if your lifestyle and mindset are unhealthy, most times, you'll fight tooth and nail to keep them that way if it's familiar. It didn't matter how much she believed in me, I didn't believe in myself. I treated her like an authority figure that wanted to change me.

Work related stress at the time wasn't helping. She was doing ad sales for a local publication and was hustling around the clock and my degenerate ass was still in the service industry. I said I was over it but it's always easy to fall back on. I was actually offered a part time gig at a brewery and decided it was in my best interests to take it. I had been working there for a couple months when I got a call from Jean's brother in law, who was my boss when I worked for their family business.

He was still in the field and had recently done a job for a crazy old lady who was looking for a chauffeur. She was practically blind and required assistance for a variety of day to day activities. Nothing medical or gross, just basic shit like shopping, checking the mail and getting around. She asked if he could recommend anyone. He knew I used to drive a taxi so he hit me up and asked if I'd be interested. It sounded unusual but it wasn't a restaurant and that sounded good enough at the time. I told him to give her my number. The next day I got a call from Ms. Rebecca Welles Weis. She asked me to come over and more or less interview for the position. She didn't live that far from me.

When I arrived, a young man who was a friend as well as her massage therapist greeted me. He was there to oversee things and feel me out. The smell of chlorine hit me as soon as I walked in. There was a good-sized swimming pool in the living room surrounded by plants and some expensive decor. Turns out Ms. Weis was doing alright for herself. She came out from the kitchen to greet me. Picture a little old Jewish lady with dark hair and way too much makeup, big flashy jewelry, white leggings and a black velvet long sleeved top that says "cougar" across it in glittery letters. That was Rebecca.

She immediately started scolding me about my tattoos. I cordially explained that I had been led to believe she was blind and didn't realize she'd be able to see them. I apologized for not showing up looking more presentable and assured her I could cover them up if need be. She had extremely poor eyesight but definitely wasn't blind. She was in her late 80's and fairly independent under the circumstances but preferred to have assistance walking if and when possible. She grabbed my hand and started giving me a tour of the house while telling me about herself. She was old Hollywood, an actress with a long resume who knew everyone from John Wayne and Steve McQueen to Lucille Ball and Marilyn Monroe. Her late husband, Don, was a director whose claim to fame were shows like M.A.S.H and the original Batman series.

If you're familiar with old James Bond movies, you probably remember the notorious villain, Dr. Blofeld. You also might remember that before you actually see him on screen, you just see his hands stroking a beautiful white Persian cat. That was Rebecca's cat. She had two of them; one was a stand in for the other. She still got royalty checks for them in the mail daily. We agreed to do a trial run and hang for a day. I was told to come by tomorrow morning and we'd play it by ear. She said she would pay me twenty dollars an hour under the table.

The next day I showed up ready to work but she wasn't in a rush to go anywhere or do anything. She more or less picked up where we left off the day before and just continued on with her crazy Hollywood stories. Rebecca loved to talk about herself. She supposedly spoke to Sharon Tate on the phone the day of the Manson family murders, attempted to hook up her late daughter with Steven Spielberg and once lived next door to Frank Sinatra. She had a downstairs garage that housed two cars, a Kia Soul for everyday life and a 1967 custom painted Ferrari red Rolls Royce Corniche for less conventional occasions. It was an original model with the steering wheel on the right hand side. I used to get priceless looks from people while driving that car.

Rebecca enjoyed cooking (to the best of her abilities) and decided she wanted to make us lunch the next day. She busted out what I still refer to today as 'pretentious pizza'. It was pita bread topped with cream cheese, salmon, tomato, arugula, a slice of lemon, and Beluga caviar, served on a Cartier plate. I used to make the poor man's version at home, minus the Beluga of course, because that shit is literally over a hundred dollars for one ounce. It's supposedly the most expensive caviar in the world. So there we are eating pretentious pizza off of Cartier plate ware and Rebecca proceeds to explain that this week is special because we'll be going to pick up a check from her lawyers office. Her brother, a successful fashion designer, sadly passed away a while back and left the remains of his fortune to her. It's been in the works for some time and it's all finally getting sorted this week.

Sure enough, a couple days later I rolled the old lady on

down to a small law office and picked up a big check, 4.3 million dollars to be exact. Have you ever held a check for 4.3 million dollars? Because I have. The way I was addressed and treated at the bank upon and after depositing that thing was pretty surreal. That same time the year before, I was unemployed and living out of my car. Now I was driving a Rolls, eating Beluga caviar and depositing huge checks for a millionaire, life is funny like that. I worked for Rebecca for about a year and although there were days where we wanted to strangle each other, we actually had a lot of good times together.

I know what you might be thinking but there's no Hollywood ending here either. She didn't leave me money or anything upon passing away a week after her 90th birthday. She had some legal issues as well as a long list of people who were already lined up for all that. Working for Rebecca actually made me appreciate the simplicity of being broke. I could tell more Rebecca stories but hey, let's get back to the dumpster fire that is my life.

Chanel and I squeezed two road trips and two leases into the fourteen months that we were together. We broke our first lease a little early for the sake of catching what we thought was an upgrade at the time. It wasn't a bad place but it would go on to be our break up house in addition to being haunted. Chanel moved out when we split and I convinced my friend, Alex to move in to take her place. I couldn't afford to stay there on my own.

Alex was a homie from way back. He moved around a little bit but was relocating to New Mexico before hitting the road again. He basically just used the crib as a storage unit, which worked for me because I didn't have much after Chanel left. We bought a lot of stuff together which basically made it hers. It wasn't spiteful, she put forth more effort to acquire things and wanted them more than I did. Alex bounced and wasn't planning on coming back for a few months. I was living alone in a furnished house with half the rent paid. It sounds cool but it totally wasn't. It was one of the worst times of my life.

I re-lived countless moments that Chanel and I spent together, I saw her in every room. I couldn't sleep and started having crazy nightmares when I actually did. Shit used to fly off the walls, not fall off —fly. I had little wooden art pieces hanging above the fireplace that seemed to just leap off of it occasionally. Like someone was throwing them. It looked and felt abnormal as fuck. Between the nightmares and flying art collection, I decided the spot was occupied by some kind of dark energy. I would light prayer candles and try and do some ceremonial shit up in there to cleanse the place but it didn't seem to work. The candles would usually go out or even break. It was creepy.

I started having difficulty being alone, especially at the house. My friend, Nikki really held me down during this time. She'd let me stay on her couch or even kick it at her crib when she was at work. She'd come chill with me even if it was a major inconvenience. I'll never forget that, thank you Nikki.

I started butting heads with my landlord when all this other bullshit was going down too. I had a gnarly insect infestation that he wasn't taking seriously amongst other things. I was so over living at this place. We agreed to peacefully part ways, I put my life (mostly Alex's life) back into a storage unit and returned to living out of my car. Regardless of the circumstances, Chanel and I attempted to get back together. I'll spare you the details but we didn't succeed. Nevertheless, I'll always be grateful that we found each other. She helped me realize that companionship is sacred and real love is rare. I took that, and her, for granted. Sometimes I wish I could go back and do it all over differently. Maybe we'll find each other again in another life.

When I was growing up I always wanted to be someone. Now I realize I should have been more specific.

—Lily Tomlin

20

$\mathfrak{I}$ could bore you with redundant tales of being homeless again for the next six months but I won't. I eventually got myself a studio and re-attained things to call my own. I quit smoking weed and cigarettes and cut back on drinking. I try to exercise, be conscious of what I eat, drink water and take my vitamins. Even when I hate myself, I try not to take it out on my body like I used too.

If you managed to read this self-indulgent quest for relevance, I hope you got something out of it. Some people told me that it was silly to try and do this by the age of thirty-three. Truth be told, I agree. But I'm pretty burnt and have difficulty remembering shit, so if I waited much longer I might not have been able to do it. My story isn't that unusual, I know folks that walked a way harder path than I did. You probably do too; I don't know anyone who had an easy ride. But I know it's easier when we ride together.

I've lost touch with a lot of people mentioned in this book but I've learned that it's never too late to make new friends. I hope I didn't offend anyone by doing this. I tried to be mindful of the stories that weren't just mine to tell. I left out a lot and did my best to not say anything negative about anyone. I didn't mention the Philadelphia trip, Jazz Fest in New Orleans, New Years in Denver, graff jams in Phoenix or the weekend in Vegas. I guess not every story needs to be shared.

I don't have a final thought or piece of parting advice for anybody. I have opinions based on my own experiences but that's about it. I like to tell myself I was being open to opportunity or dare I say destiny by moving around and making spontaneous, poorly thought out decisions. I thought at one point if I stuck to my guns, the universe would reward me for doing so. It's a nice thought but again, this is real life and we can't all be extraordinary. But I do admire those that try. Life is an astonishing gift, I wanted to utilize and explore, take risks and go against the odds.

Have you ever heard the story about how Dr. Seuss got his first cartoon published? He was supposedly coming from a publishing office where his work had been rejected for like, the twenty seventh time. It's been said that he was going home to burn it and had decided to go into the dry cleaning business. He happened to run into an old buddy on the way, who had just taken a job as editor for children's books at Vanguard. One thing led to another and voila, Dr. Fucking Seuss. Years later, he said that if he had perhaps been walking on the other side of the street that day, things might have turned out differently for him. I love those kinds of stories; I always hoped I could tell my own one day. I was steadily looking for that right place, right time moment, hoping I was on the right side of the street. But I'm no Dr. Seuss.

I haven't changed much since I was a kid. I still like graffiti and rap, still like my clothes kind of big, still use slang in my every day speech, still like a good night out. Although these days it's more common for me to be posted at home with an autobiography, more interesting than this one.

That being said, I still couldn't tell you what I'll be doing a year from now. Maybe I'm a loser, or a free spirit, maybe you can't really be one without the other. I'll probably always be a kind of a kid with my head in the clouds. I'm currently writing this on an airplane from California back to New Mexico. I figured I would wrap this up at a beach or a restaurant counter while downing my fourth cup of coffee but I suppose it's fitting that I'm doing it in the sky. It's nighttime. I enjoy night flights for whatever reason. I'm sitting next to an elderly gentleman who greeted me before take off.

> *"How's it going?"*
> "Well, thank you, how about yourself?"
> *"Very well."*
> "Cool, where ya headed?"
> *"Dallas, I'm going to see my grandkids."*
> "That's great!"
> *"And you? Where are you off to young man?"*
> "That's a good question, who knows…"

end

www.ingramcontent.com/pod-product-compliance
Lightning Source LLC
Chambersburg PA
CBHW031501120626
46545CB00005B/1700